Microsoft Dynamics CRM 2011: Dashboards Cookbook

Over 50 simple but incredibly effective recipes for creating, customizing, and interacting with rich dashboards and charts

Mark AuCoin

[PACKT] enterprise

PUBLISHING

professional expertise distilled

BIRMINGHAM - MUMBAI

Microsoft Dynamics CRM 2011: Dashboards Cookbook

First published: January 2012

Production Reference: 1120112

Published by Packt Publishing Ltd.
Livery Place
35 Livery Street
Birmingham B3 2PB, UK.

ISBN 978-1-84968-440-8

www.packtpub.com

Cover Image by John Green (iguana@cogeco.ca)

Credits

Author

Mark AuCoin

Reviewers

Daniel Cai

Richard Knudson

Mohamed Ibrahim Mostafa

Nicolae Tarla

Acquisition Editor

Stephanie Moss

Lead Technical Editor

Hyacintha D'Souza

Technical Editors

Mehreen Shaikh

Azharuddin Sheikh

Project Coordinator

Jovita Pinto

Proofreader

Chris Smith

Indexer

Rekha Nair

Production Coordinator

Alwin Roy

Cover Work

Alwin Roy

About the Author

Mark AuCoin is a Microsoft MVP and Senior CRM Solution Specialist for Navantis, which won the 2010 and 2011 CRM Solution Partner of the Year award from Microsoft Canada. Mark has been in the software industry since 1992 and has been involved in many different projects and technologies over that time. Starting out in client/server and ERP systems then migrating to the Internet and leveraging years of database and reporting skills he focused on building business-class web-enabled systems. Then Mark was introduced to Microsoft Dynamics CRM. He was impressed with the ability to focus more on the business requirements and "what" needs to get done instead of worrying so much about "how" it was going to get done. Since diving into Dynamics CRM in 2006, Mark has been involved in bringing a Dynamics CRM mobile solution to market, became a speaker at Dynamics CRM events, and has attained Microsoft Virtual Technical Specialist status for Dynamics CRM in Canada.

Mark has a techinal blog at `http://crmmongrel.blogspot.com`.

I would like to thank Joe AuCoin and Gurt Pawan for their support when I was getting started with Dynamics CRM. Your business experience and guidance was invaluable to me, thank you. I would also like to thank John Kvasnic, Kevin Oakes, and the whole Navantis team for being such a great company that people are really proud to be a part of. The Management team has vision, the Sales team are all top professionals and the Development groups are simply amazing. Lastly, I would also like to thank the Dynamics CRM community, which includes the numerous bloggers and speakers that I follow. This book wouldn't be possible without the countless articles and snippets that helped me along the way. The community is driving the product forward with timely articles and enhancements that are based on real-world experience.

About the Reviewers

Daniel Cai is an independent consultant specializing in Microsoft Dynamics CRM, .NET, and Business Intelligence solution development. He has years of professional experience in designing, developing, and delivering large-scale enterprise applications.

Daniel is a Microsoft Dynamics CRM MVP, and the founder of Tata Solutions, a specialized IT solution provider offering full-cycle Microsoft Dynamics CRM development and consulting services.

Daniel is a holder of several professional certificates including MCP, MCSE, MCDBA, MCSD, MCTS for Microsoft Dynamics CRM, and SCJP.

Daniel has a technical blog at `http://danielcai.blogspot.com`.

Mohamed Ibrahim Mostafa is a Technical Solutions Architect and Senior Consultant at CIBER. Mohamed comes with extensive Microsoft Dynamics CRM experience having worked on a large number of CRM implementations for projects of various sizes helping clients from different business sectors to implement successful solutions based on the platform. Mohamed is certified in Microsoft Dynamics CRM 3.0, CRM 4.0, and CRM 2011. He also comes with long experience in leading development teams and projects, and designing and architecting solutions with strong client-focused Consultancy skills. Mohamed is certified in several other Microsoft technologies and he is a most valuable professional (MVP) in Scribe Software.

Nicolae Tarla is a Senior Consultant with Navantis Inc. He is working with enterprise clients in America and Canada. Nicolae is focused on designing and implementing enterprise solutions for CRM, SharePoint and related .NET technologies. He is an integral part of the CRM community, contributing through his blog at `nicolaet.wordpress.com`.

Nicolae can be reached at `nicolae.tarla@live.com`.

I first want to thank Mark for giving me the opportunity to assist him with this project. He is always a source of inspiration. Of course, I want to thank my wife and daughter for supporting me and patiently accepting my extended hours of tinkering.

www.PacktPub.com

Support files, eBooks, discount offers and more

You might want to visit www.PacktPub.com for support files and downloads related to your book.

Did you know that Packt offers eBook versions of every book published, with PDF and ePub files available? You can upgrade to the eBook version at www.PacktPub.com and as a print book customer, you are entitled to a discount on the eBook copy. Get in touch with us at service@packtpub.com for more details.

At www.PacktPub.com, you can also read a collection of free technical articles, sign up for a range of free newsletters and receive exclusive discounts and offers on Packt books and eBooks.

 PACKTLIB®

http://PacktLib.PacktPub.com

Do you need instant solutions to your IT questions? PacktLib is Packt's online digital book library. Here, you can access, read and search across Packt's entire library of books.

Why Subscribe?

- ▸ Fully searchable across every book published by Packt
- ▸ Copy and paste, print and bookmark content
- ▸ On demand and accessible via web browser

Free Access for Packt account holders

If you have an account with Packt at www.PacktPub.com, you can use this to access PacktLib today and view nine entirely free books. Simply use your login credentials for immediate access.

Instant Updates on New Packt Books

Get notified! Find out when new books are published by following @PacktEnterprise on Twitter, or the *Packt Enterprise* Facebook page.

I would like to dedicate this book to my wife Bernadette. Thank you for putting up with all the late hours and never complaining once.

Table of Contents

Preface

This cookbook is full of practical and easily applicable recipes that will teach the user how to understand and unleash the full capabilities of the new dashboard features in Microsoft Dynamics CRM 2011. Starting with basic tasks to build user confidence and general knowledge, the chapters provide insight with helpful tips and related content. The book moves on to more advanced topics around charting and extending with components to help the user visually transform their business data using colors, drill-downs, and dynamic content.

What this book covers

Chapter 1, Viewing Dashboards, introduces the concept of a dashboard in Dynamics CRM 2011. The reader will learn how to locate dashboards, set default dashboards, and review the standard dashboards that come with Dynamics CRM 2011.

Chapter 2, Interacting with Dashboards, covers the types of interactions available using charts and lists that are being displayed on a dashboard. Features including drill-downs, tooltips, and filtering and searching records are also covered.

Chapter 3, Creating a Dashboard, includes recipes that cover every step needed to create and modify a new dashboard. Adding and editing chart and list components are also included.

Chapter 4, Sharing and Assigning Dashboards, profiles dashboard security. User dashboards can be shared or assigned to other users, and this chapter goes into greater details of user dashboards.

Chapter 5, Editing and Deleting Dashboards, covers editing a user or system dashboard, along with instructions on how to publish the changes. Deleting user and system dashboards, including the effects on existing system users, is also covered.

Chapter 6, Adding IFrames and WebResources to Dashboards, covers IFrames and WebResource components that can be part of a dashboard, along with charts and lists, and provides descriptions and best practice hints.

Chapter 7, Advanced Dashboards, is focused on the dashboard itself, not the components. This chapter reviews the underlying markup language and how to modify it in order to stretch the limits of what is possible with dashboards in Dynamics CRM 2011. The Dashboard Reporting control from Microsoft is also covered in this chapter.

Chapter 8, Creating a Chart, reviews the latest version of Dynamics CRM 2011 and teaches the user how to create their own charts, including some real-world examples because charts are a big part of the dashboard experience.

Chapter 9, Advanced Chart XML, shows how to export, modify, and import a chart for Dynamics CRM 2011. Special undocumented features are covered, teaching the user to create compelling charts and use FetchXML to control the data.

Appendix, Dashboard Examples, provides a few examples of dashboards targeted towards sales, service, and marketing groups. The charts and components shown on the dashboards use the techniques described earlier in the earlier chapters.

What you need for this book

In order to complete the recipes provided in this book, the reader will need a Windows PC that is running Microsoft Internet Explorer (latest version) with full access to the Internet. The reader will not need a deep technical background for the majority of the chapters, but some of the later chapters assume the reader is experienced with XML and the concepts of FetchXML. For the later *advanced* chapters, the user will need an XML editor such as Microsoft Visual Studio in order to complete the recipes.

Who this book is for

If you are a developer who is excited about creating, customizing, and designing dashboards in Dynamics CRM 2011, this book is for you. You should be comfortable with general Dynamics CRM functionality for this or a previous release. This book may also be valuable to end users and power users interested in the new dashboard features of this release.

Conventions

In this book, you will find a number of styles of text that distinguish between different kinds of information. Here are some examples of these styles, and an explanation of their meaning.

Code words in text are shown as follows: "We can include other contexts through the use of the `include` directive."

A block of code is set as follows:

```
<table>
  <tbody>
    <tr>
      <td>Enter Area Code:</td>
      <td><input name="txtAreaCode"></td>
      <td><input onclick="doSearch()" value="Search"
           type="button"></td>
    </tr>
  </tbody>
</table>
```

When we wish to draw your attention to a particular part of a code block, the relevant lines or items are set in bold:

```
<category alias="_CRMAutoGen_groupby_column_Num_0">
  <measurecollection>
    <measure alias="_CRMAutoGen_aggregate_column_Num_0" />
  </measurecollection>
  <measurecollection>
    <measure alias="aggregate_column2" />
  </measurecollection>
</category>
```

New terms and **important words** are shown in bold. Words that you see on the screen, in menus or dialog boxes for example, appear in the text like this: "Navigate to the **Customizations** section in the Dynamics CRM 2011 **Settings** area."

Warnings or important notes appear in a box like this.

Tips and tricks appear like this.

Reader feedback

Feedback from our readers is always welcome. Let us know what you think about this book—what you liked or may have disliked. Reader feedback is important for us to develop titles that you really get the most out of.

To send us general feedback, simply send an e-mail to feedback@packtpub.com, and mention the book title through the subject of your message.

If there is a topic that you have expertise in and you are interested in either writing or contributing to a book, see our author guide on www.packtpub.com/authors.

Customer support

Now that you are the proud owner of a Packt book, we have a number of things to help you to get the most from your purchase.

Downloading the example code

You can download the example code files for all Packt books you have purchased from your account at http://www.packtpub.com. If you purchased this book elsewhere, you can visit http://www.packtpub.com/support and register to have the files e-mailed directly to you.

Errata

Although we have taken every care to ensure the accuracy of our content, mistakes do happen. If you find a mistake in one of our books—maybe a mistake in the text or the code—we would be grateful if you would report this to us. By doing so, you can save other readers from frustration and help us improve subsequent versions of this book. If you find any errata, please report them by visiting http://www.packtpub.com/support, selecting your book, clicking on the **errata submission form** link, and entering the details of your errata. Once your errata are verified, your submission will be accepted and the errata will be uploaded to our website, or added to any list of existing errata, under the Errata section of that title.

Piracy

Piracy of copyright material on the Internet is an ongoing problem across all media. At Packt, we take the protection of our copyright and licenses very seriously. If you come across any illegal copies of our works, in any form, on the Internet, please provide us with the location address or website name immediately so that we can pursue a remedy.

Please contact us at copyright@packtpub.com with a link to the suspected pirated material.

We appreciate your help in protecting our authors, and our ability to bring you valuable content.

Questions

You can contact us at questions@packtpub.com if you are having a problem with any aspect of the book, and we will do our best to address it.

1
Viewing Dashboards

In this chapter, we will cover:

- ► Creating a free Dynamics CRM 2011 Online account
- ► Finding and selecting dashboards
- ► Expanding and collapsing dashboard sections
- ► Changing your default CRM 2011 Dashboard
- ► Making Dashboards your CRM 2011 homepage

Introduction

One of the best user features found in Dynamics CRM 2011 is the addition of standard dashboards. Dashboards can contain any combination of charts, lists, and other components to help give users a visual and interactive view of their CRM data.

At first glance, dashboards and their myriad information can be overwhelming to some users who are new to the Dynamics CRM 2011 interface. This chapter will guide you through the basics of navigating between dashboards and setting some basic personal options. We finish up by reviewing the standard CRM 2011 Dashboards with an explanation of what data is represented on these dashboards.

Creating a free Dynamics CRM 2011 Online account

In order to learn about the basics of viewing and later modifying dashboards in Dynamics CRM 2011, it is suggested that you create a free 30-day trial account for Dynamics CRM 2011 Online. In this way, you will be free to explore and test out the many features of CRM 2011 without any risk of being exposed to the production environment.

Getting ready

You need to have an active Microsoft Windows Live ID in order to register for a free 30-day trial account with Dynamics CRM 2011 Online. If you do not have a Windows Live ID yet, you should visit https://signup.live.com/ to sign up. You can create a Windows Live ID by using your existing e-mail address, or by requesting a new Hotmail address. There is timely communication about features and the status of your CRM Online instance during the 30 days of trial, so make sure to check the e-mail address you used to sign-up for the trial for important tips.

How to do it...

Creating a Microsoft Dynamics CRM 2011 Online instance can be accomplished in under 20 minutes. Keep your organization name and e-mail address ready before you begin. This instanced of CRM Online can be used to complete all the recipes found in this book.

1. Visit the http://crm.dynamics.com/ website and click on the large **GET STARTED!** button in the **Free Trial** section as shown in the following screenshot:

2. You will be taken to an overview page that provides information about features found in CRM 2011 and how the 30-day trial account works. When you are finished reading, click on the **TRY NOW!** button as shown in the following screenshot:

3. Now you can begin to set up your free 30-day trial account. **Step 1** is the **Country/Region** information: this might already be selected based on your IE settings. Change the country if it is incorrect, and provide an active e-mail address in the **E-mail** field and click on the **Next** button as shown in the following screenshot:

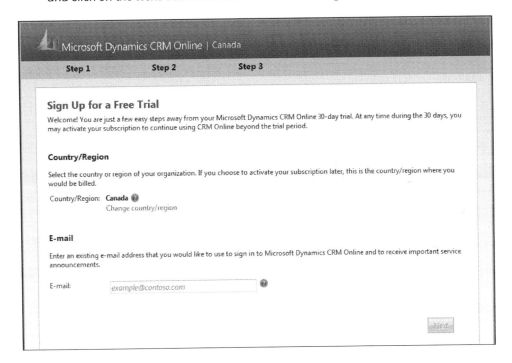

4. Sign in by using your Windows Live ID (e-mail address and password). Click on the **Sign in** button. This e-mail account automatically becomes the billing administrator and is the only account that Microsoft will use to process your request if you wish to turn your trial into a full subscription. There is no self-serve method to change this later and you will have to contact Microsoft directly to perform the change for you.

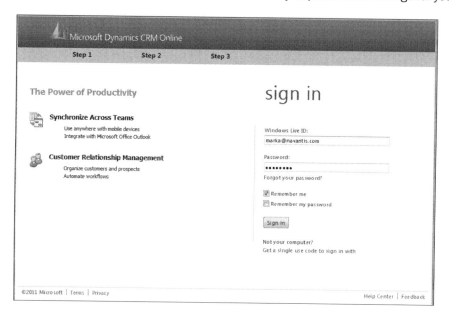

5. Provide the CAPTCHA characters to ensure the safety of the service. Read through and accept the terms of service. Click on the **Next** button as shown in the following screenshot:

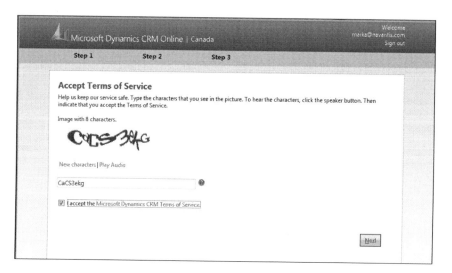

6. Complete the **Sign-up** form by providing the contact and company information.

7. Click on the **Finish** button.

8. Microsoft Dynamics CRM Online will now provision a new account for you. Leave the window open, as this might take a few minutes to complete. When it is done, you will see the following screen:

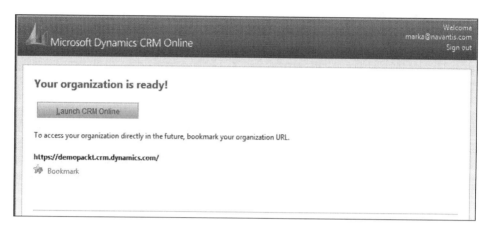

9. From this screen, you can create a bookmark by clicking on the **Bookmark** link shown in the preceding screenshot. The URL for your account will probably contain the organization name you entered in **Step 3** of the sign-up process. Clicking on the **Launch CRM Online** button will take you to your CRM 2011 Online account, where you can now begin to tackle some tasks.

How it works...

Dynamics CRM 2011 is a Software-As-A-Service-based solution running from the Microsoft Azure cloud. When you sign up for a new Dynamics CRM 2011 Online account, a new instance of Dynamics CRM is provisioned in the Azure cloud environment.

There's more...

An important thing to point out about the **Company Name** field is that the value you provide cannot be changed later on. I would suggest using something similar to demoMyCompany (where MyCompany is your organization name). **Country**, **Currency**, and **Language** cannot be changed after sign-up, and they may affect pricing and offers from Microsoft if you decide to turn the trial account into a paid account later on.

You will receive an e-mail from Microsoft with the URL for your new instance of Dynamics CRM 2011 Online. However, if you ever lose or forget the URL, you can go to the main http://crm.dynamics.com/ website and click on the **CUSTOMER SIGN IN** link located in the top menu section.

Finding and selecting dashboards

The Microsoft Dynamics CRM 2011 interface has many new buttons, links, and UI features that can be a bit overwhelming at first glance. This section will introduce you to some of the common navigation methods to locate and view different dashboards.

Getting ready

Sign in to your Microsoft Dynamics 2011 Online account (we created one in the first section) by using your Windows Live ID credentials. By default, the Dynamics CRM 2011 application already has the Dashboards area set as the homepage. Therefore, the first time you sign into the application, you will start with the Dashboards. Microsoft Dynamics CRM Online comes ready with pre-populated sample data. This data will help you to build your dashboards, and is the same as is used in the rest of this book.

How to do it...

Carry out the following steps in order to complete this recipe:

1. By default, the **Dashboards** link can be found in the **Workplace** section of the left-hand navigation for Dynamics CRM 2011, as shown in the following screenshot:

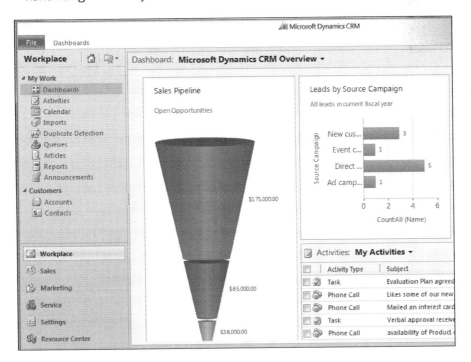

2. When working in the **Dashboard** area, you can select a different dashboard by clicking on the small down arrrow next to the current dashboard's title and then choosing a new dashboard to view. The following screenshot shows one such example of this:

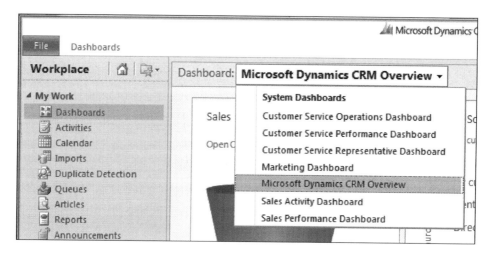

3. Another way to select and view dashboards is by clicking on the similar small arrow when you highlight the **Dashboards** link in the left-hand navigation section, as depicted in the following screenshtot:

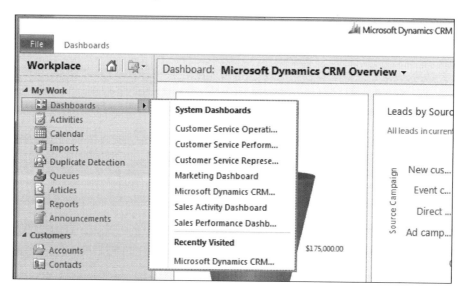

4. One of the new navigation features in Dynamics CRM 2011 is the new **Recently Visited** and **Favorites** link; this lets you quickly jump to a dashboard when you are not in the **Workplace** section. You can also **pin** your favorite dashboards, so that they are always available. For example, the following screenshot shows how you can access a favorite dashboard while you are still in the **Sales** section.

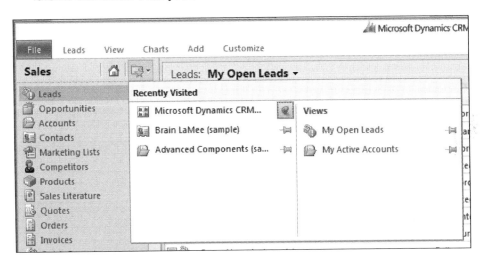

There's more...

Now that you understand the basics around locating and viewing CRM Dashboards, let's take a detailed look at the standard dashboards that come with the Dynamics CRM 2011 application and what each one contains.

To review each standard Dashboard, sign in to your Dynamics CRM 2011 Online account and navigate to the **Dashboards** section in the **Workplace** area.

Microsoft Dynamics CRM Overview Dashboard

The **Microsoft Dynamics CRM Overview Dashboard** is a good example of how a general user who might work across multiple modules in CRM (*Sales, Marketing & Service*) can use a dashboard to get a view of the entire system.

▶ The **Sales Pipeline** chart is a funnel report on *open/active* opportunity records, grouped into the different stages.

▶ The **Leads by Source Campaign** chart shows all lead records that came in as a direct result of a CRM-managed campaign. The data is grouped by campaign and covers the current fiscal year.

▶ The **Cases By Priority (Per Day)** chart is a stacked chart that tracks the active cases assigned to the current user per day, stacked by priority.

▸ The list of **My Activities** is a collection of CRM Activities (**Phone Call**, **Task**, **Appointment**, **Email**, and so on) that belong to the current user.

These are depicted in the following screenshot:

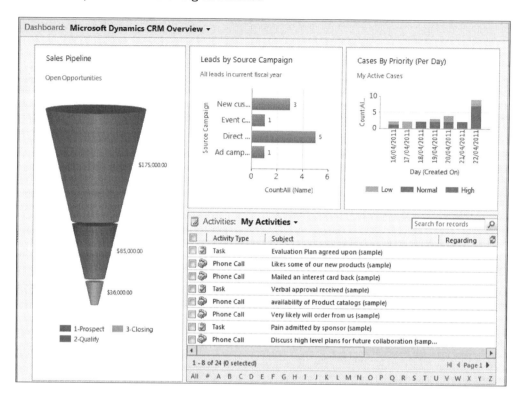

Sales Activity Dashboard

The **Sales Activity Dashboard** is an example of how a sales person might design a dashboard. The idea is to provide sales data and goal measurements to quickly identify areas that need attention. All the charts are focused on the current user's data.

▸ The **Sales Pipeline** chart is a funnel report on open/active opportunity records, grouped into the different stages.

▸ The **Percentage Achieved** chart shows the progress against the user's active goals. These goals cover four quarters of the current fiscal period, and track opportunities.

▸ The **Leads by Source** chart shows all the Lead records this user owns, and groups them by source (**Advertisement**, **Trade Show**, **Referral** and so on).

▸ The **Top Opportunities** chart takes the user's list of open opportunities and selects the top 10 based on the estimated revenue.

▶ The **Top Customers** chart takes the user's list of closed opportunities for the current fiscal period and selects the top ten opportunities based on the estimated revenue. The related customer name is also displayed.

▶ The list of **My Activities** is a collection of CRM Activities (**Phone Call**, **Task**, **Appointment**, **Email**, and so on) that belong to the current user.

These are depicted in the following screenshot:

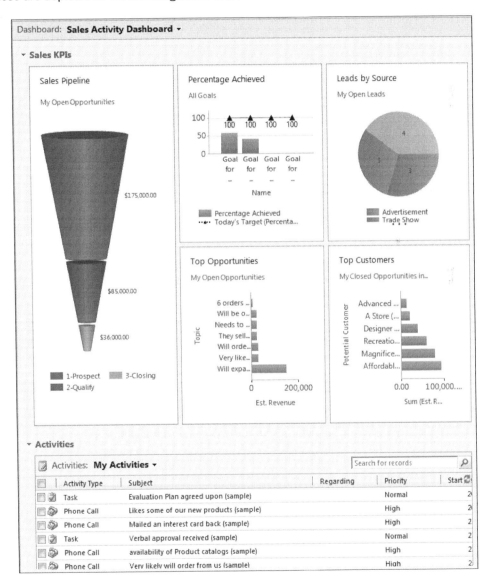

Sales Performance Dashboard

The **Sales Performance Dashboard** shows how a manager or VP can use a dashboard to view the progress of a team or the entire organization. The charts read data across the entire CRM system, not just for the current user account.

- ▸ The **Sales Pipeline** chart is a funnel report on open/active opportunity records, grouped into the different stages.

- ▸ The **Goals Progress (Money)** chart allows the user to see how the team or organization is progressing towards financial goals. This example uses opportunities grouped by fiscal quarters.

- ▸ The **Percentage Achieved** chart shows the progress against active goals. The default goals cover four quarters of the current fiscal period, tracking opportunities.

- ▸ The **Sales Leaderboard** chart sums opportunities closed in this fiscal period and groups them by the opportunity owner.

- ▸ The **Deals Won vs. Deals Lost By Owner** is a stacked chart that sums the opportunities won in this fiscal period and combines that with a sum of the opportunities lost in this fiscal period. That data is then grouped by the owner of the opportunities.

These are depicted in the following screenshot:

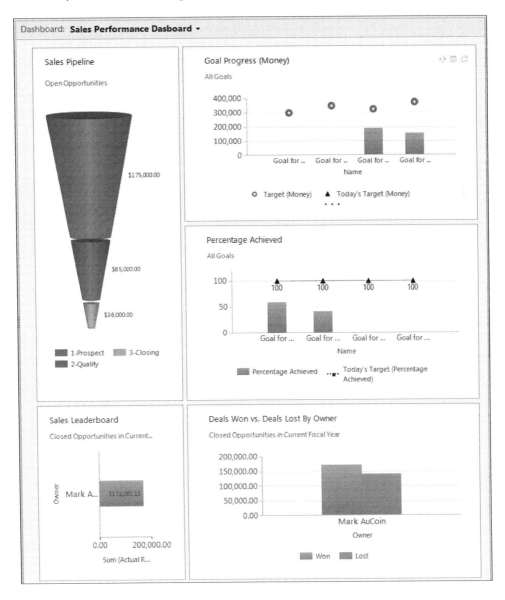

Marketing Dashboard

The **Marketing Dashboard** provides an overview of the marketing efforts across the organization. The charts presented here are more reflective rather than a call to action, but completing marketing and sales processes in CRM brings this dashboard to life.

▸ The **Campaign Type Mix** is a pie chart that simply groups all the campaigns for the current fiscal year by the campaign type field.

▸ The **Campaign Budget vs**. **Actual Costs** is a stacked chart that takes all campaigns for the current fiscal year and compares the budgeted amount versus the actual costs recorded to run the campaign. This data is then grouped by fiscal quarters.

▸ The **Leads by Source Campaign** allows the user to see the number leads generated by each campaign run in the current fiscal year. This information is driven from the new lead records that are tied back to an originating campaign.

▸ The **Revenue Generated by Campaign** chart sums the actual revenue data from all the closed opportunities for the current fiscal year and relates them back to a campaign that influenced or started the deal. This data is then grouped by campaign.

▸ The list of **My Activities** is a collection of CRM Activities (**Phone Call**, **Task**, **Appointment**, **Email**, and so on) that belong to the current user.

These are depicted in the following screenshot:

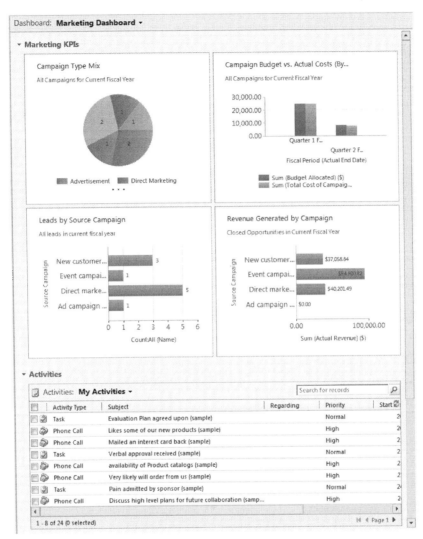

Customer Service Representative Dashboard

The **Customer Service Representative Dashboard** shows the KPIs for a Customer Service Rep, or support personnel. The chart provides case data and goal measurements to provide a quick status report. The charts are focused on data for the current user.

> ► The **Case Mix (By Origin)** is a pie chart that groups active cases by the case origin field value.

> ► **Cases By Priority (Per Day)** is a stacked chart that provides a view of the incoming cases, grouped per day, and stacked by priority.

▶ The **Case Resolution Trend (By Day)** chart is a mixed chart (bar and line) that is used to report on the number of cases closed per day, along with the average time spent to resolve those cases.

▶ The **Goal Progress (Count)** chart uses the goals data in CRM to report on numeric (count) goals instead of the usual financial goals. This chart has a target for completing cases per quarter, and shows the completed status along with a forecast for current progress towards the goal.

▶ The list of **My Activities** is a collection of CRM Activities (**Phone Call**, **Task**, **Appointment**, **Email**, and so on) that belong to the current user.

These are depicted in the following screenshot:

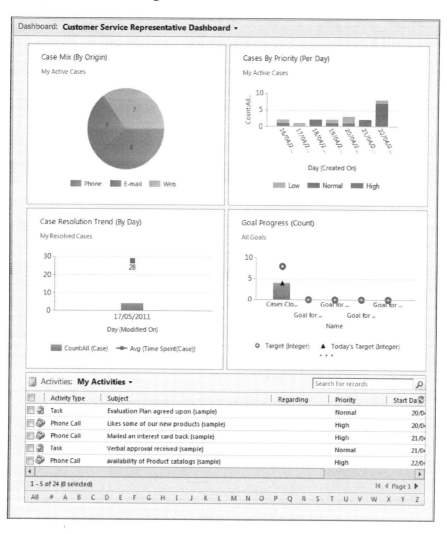

Customer Service Performance Dashboard

The **Customer Service Performance Dashboard** shows the KPIs for a customer service team within the Customer Service group. The data includes team-wide results, not just data for the current user.

- The **Service Leaderboard** chart shows the number of cases resolved in the last 7 days, grouped by the user who resolved the cases.

- The **Case Resolution Trend (By Day)** chart is a mixed chart (bar and line) that is used to report on the number of cases closed per day, along with the average time spent to resolve those cases.

- The **Goal Progress (Count)** chart uses the Goals data in CRM to report on numeric (count) goals instead of the usual financial goals. This chart has a target for completing cases per quarter, and shows the completed status along with a forecast for current progress towards the goal.

- The **Articles By Status** chart reports counts all of the knowledgebase articles stored in CRM and groups them by status (draft, unapproved, approved).

These are depicted in the following screenshot:

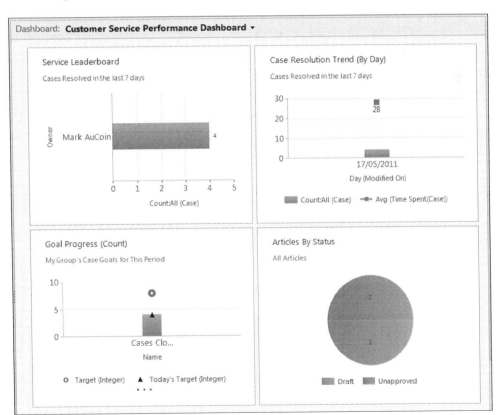

Customer Service Operations Dashboard

The Customer Service Operations Dashboard is similar to the Customer Service Performance Dashboard, except that this dashboard focuses on the entire Customer Service group (operation) and not just a team or an individual user.

- **Activities by Owner and Priority** is a stacked chart that counts open activities by the user and then stacks them by the activity priority field value.

- The **Service Leaderboard** counts all resolved cases and groups them by the user who resolved the case.

- **Articles By Status** is a pie chart that counts all of the unpublished knowledgebase articles stored in CRM and groups them by status (draft or unapproved).

- The **Cases By Origin (Per Day)** chart is a stacked chart that counts and groups all cases opened over the last 7 days and stacks them by the case source field (web, e-mail, phone).

- **Cases By Priority (Per Day)** is another stacked chart that counts and groups all active cases opened in the last 7 days and stacks them by the case priority field.

These are depicted in the following screenshot:

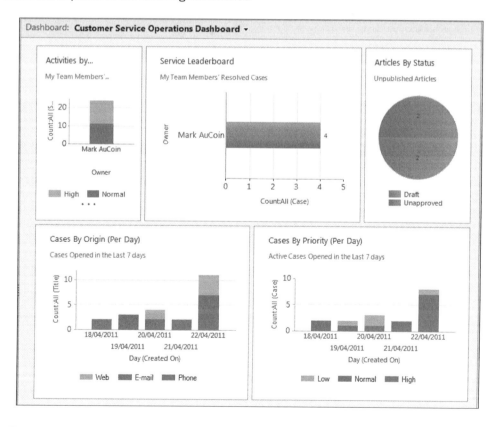

Expanding and collapsing dashboard sections

Dashboards in Dynamics CRM 2011 can be filled with many different sets of data. To help organize this information better, some dashboard layouts come with expandable and collapsible sections. Not all the layouts support collapsing sections, so we will focus on one of the standard dashboards that do. For more information, the *Creating a user dashboard* recipe in *Chapter 3, Creating a Dashboard* provides more detailed information about which dashboard layouts support collapsing sections.

Getting ready

Start by going to the **Dashboards** section in the Dynamics CRM 2011 **Workplace** area.

How to do it...

Carry out the following in order to complete this recipe:

1. From the Dynamics CRM 2011 **Workplace** area, select the **Dashboards** link.

2. Select **Marketing Dashboard** from the list of available standard dashboards, as shown in the following screenshot:

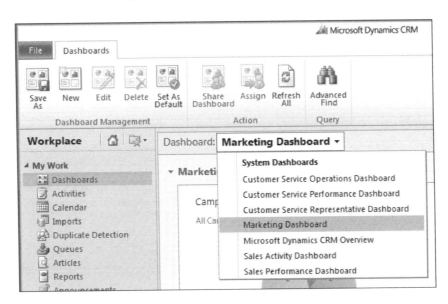

3. **Marketing Dashboard** is a large dashboard that requires the user to scroll down to view all the contents. Scroll down the screen and you will find three sections named **Marketing KPIs**, **Activities**, and **Campaigns**.

4. Single-click on the title of the first section, **Marketing KPIs**, to toggle the section's visibility.

There's more...

You will notice that when you reopen a **Dashboard** section, if there are charts displayed in that section they will be refreshed (reloaded) to show the latest data.

Changing your default CRM 2011 Dashboard

The CRM Administrator(s) have the ability to set the system-wide default dashboard for all users—the dashboard which all users see when visiting the **Dashboards** section. However, in CRM 2011, users have the ability to override this default and select a different dashboard as their personal default.

Getting ready

Launch your Dynamics CRM 2011 application. The first time you access a new Dynamics CRM 2011 environment the default dashboard will probably be the **Microsoft Dynamics CRM Overview** dashboard.

How to do it...

Carry out the following steps:

1. From the **Workplace** area in Dynamics CRM 2011, select the **Dashboards** link.

2. The system default dashboard will be displayed. It is probably the **Microsoft Dynamics CRM Overview** dashboard. If not, don't worry, the procedure is the same.

3. Select a different dashboard from the available list. In the following example, the **Sales Activity Dashboard** has been selected:

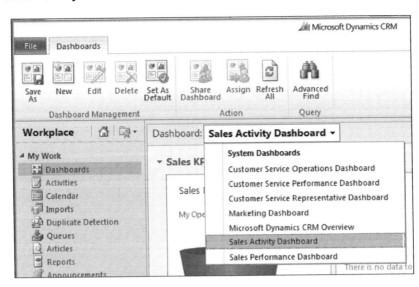

4. As this is not currently the default dashboard, there is a button available in the CRM ribbon (toolbar) named **Set As Default**, as shown in the following screenshot:

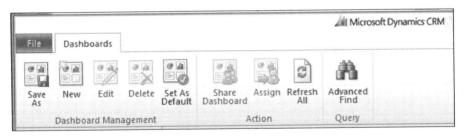

5. Click on the **Set As Default** button. If the current dashboard is already flagged as the default, then the **Set As Default** button will be disabled, as shown in the following screenshot:

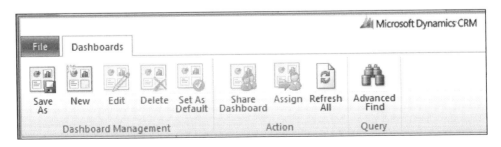

6. In order to test out the feature, click on the **Activities** section link located just beneath the Dashboards link in the **Workplace** area. Then, click again on the **Dashboards** link and you should be taken to your new default dashboard.

How it works...

Personalization settings, such as the default dashboard, are stored at the user level for Dynamics CRM 2011. The user's personalization settings override the system default settings. This applies to dashboards as well. If a user removes their personal dashboard, the system default will take effect again.

There's more...

Why doesn't the **Dashboards** link go back to my default dashboard? You may have noticed that when you navigate away from the dashboard (say into the Sales section) and then return, Dynamics CRM may not show your default dashboard, but rather goes to the last visited dashboard.

This is not a bug. CRM 2011 tries to remember your recent visits, including views and dashboards. Therefore, the default dashboard might not always be shown during your CRM session. However, if you close your browser and start a new session with Dynamics CRM 2011, the default dashboard will be shown again.

Making Dashboards your CRM 2011 homepage

Another personalization setting found in Dynamics CRM 2011 is the ability to set where your homepage link will lead. In this recipe, we will ensure that it lands on the **Dashboards** section.

Getting ready

Launch the Dynamics CRM 2011 application. You don't need to be in any particular section (Workplace, Sales, and so on) for this recipe.

How to do it...

Carry out the following steps in order to complete this recipe:

1. From the Dynamics CRM 2011 interface, find the **File** menu tab at the top of the CRM application window. Click the **Options** menu item as shown in the following screenshot:

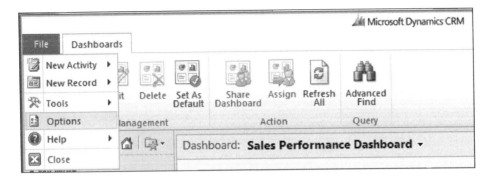

2. A dialog named **Set Personal Options** will appear with eight tabs along the top. Select the **General** tab.

3. At the top of this tab, you will see a picklist named **Default Pane**; make sure this is set to **Workplace** as shown in the following screenshot:

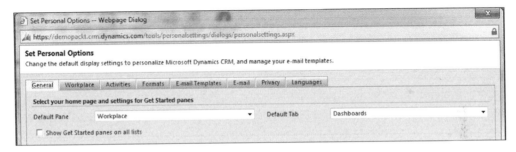

4. In the section picklist called **Default Tab**, select **Dashboards**.

5. Click on the **OK** button at the bottom right of the **Set Personal Options** dialog. This will cause your Dynamics CRM interface to refresh and apply any changes that have been made. The **Workplace** and **Dashboards** area will be the default location for you homepage link.

I don't have a Workplace or a Dashboard section

If you are missing the **Workplace** or **Dashboards** section in your Dynamics CRM navigation, chances are that the system sitemap for Dynamics CRM 2011 has been modified by your CRM Administrators. They may have been removed or renamed. If this is the case, then you should contact your CRM Administrator for assistance in finding the **Dashboards** section.

2
Interacting with Dashboards

In this chapter, we will cover:

- ▸ Enlarging a chart to full screen
- ▸ Using the tooltips on a chart
- ▸ Refreshing dashboard data
- ▸ Drilling down into a chart
- ▸ Working with inline charts and filtered records
- ▸ Searching for records in a list
- ▸ Sorting records in a list
- ▸ Filtering records in a list
- ▸ Changing the view for a dashboard list

Introduction

Building on our experiences from the first chapter, this chapter will delve into some of the unique interactions that are available in the chart and list components that can be used on dashboards in Dynamics CRM 2011.

Enlarging a chart to full screen

Navigating through the different dashboards that come with Dynamics CRM 2011, as we did in *Chapter 1, Viewing Dashboards*, you have seen many different variations on how to view chart data. When too many charts are added to a dashboard, things can be a bit congested. In order to focus directly on one chart item and see things in a greater detail, there is an **Enlarge the chart** option.

Getting ready

Start by going to the **Dashboards** section in the Dynamics CRM 2011 **Workplace** area.

How to do it...

Carry out the following steps in order to complete this recipe:

1. Select the **Dashboards** link from the **Workplace** area.

2. Select the **Microsoft Dynamics CRM Overview** dashboard as shown in the following screenshot:

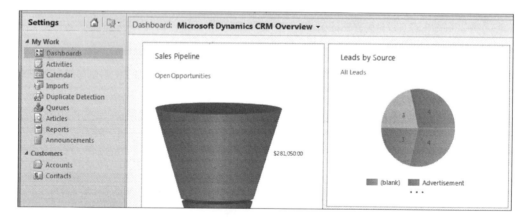

3. Locate the **Sales Pipeline funnel** chart on this dashboard, hover with the mouse cursor over the upper right-hand corner of the chart, and a small three-item menu will appear. In the following screenshot, you can see the **Enlarge the chart** option highlighted:

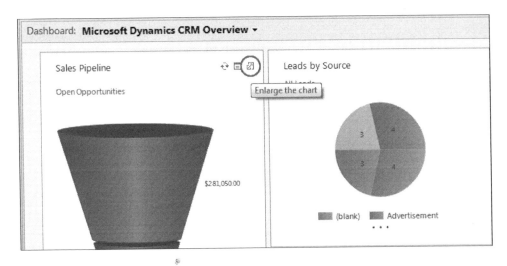

4. Click on this menu option to enlarge this dashboard chart. The chart will expand to take all of the available space in the dashboard, hiding all other dashboard elements as shown in the following screenshot:

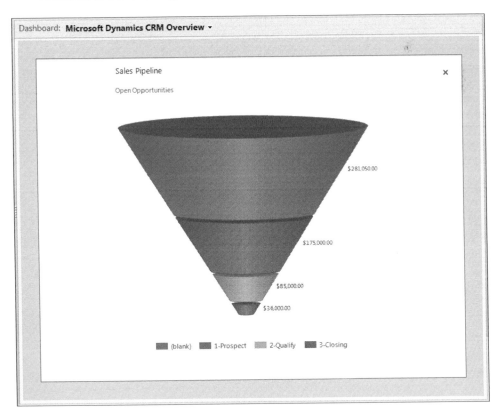

5. In order to close the enlarged view of the chart, click on the **x** located in the upper right-hand corner of the dashboard, as highlighted in the following screenshot. You will return to the main view of the **Microsoft Dynamics CRM Overview** dashboard:

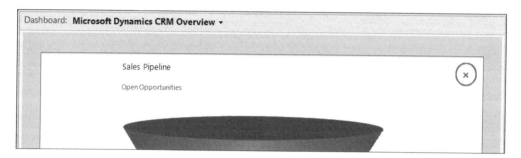

 All charts displayed on a Dynamics CRM 2011 dashboard can be enlarged. However, other dashboard components such as lists (covered later in this chapter) do not have this ability.

Using the tooltips on a chart

Charts are an excellent way to view data as they allow users to graphically represent data. Charts can display multiple data series, and then compare or contrast the results. Occasionally, viewing large sets of graphical data can become difficult as there might be too many data points to read at the same time. In order to help users make sense of the data, the Dynamics CRM 2011 charts include the **tooltips** feature.

Getting ready

Navigate to the **Dashboards** section in the Dynamics CRM 2011 **Workplace** area.

How to do it...

Carry out the following steps in order to complete this recipe:

1. Select the **Dashboards** link from the **Workplace** area.

2. Select the **Microsoft Dynamics CRM Overview** dashboard.

3. By using the **Sales Pipeline** chart (which shows all the user's open opportunity records, grouped by sales stage), place your mouse cursor over one of the **segments** of the funnel.

4. This will bring up a tooltip that provides information on that segment. In the following screenshot, you can see the tooltip being shown for the red segment. The information informs the user that they have **$175,000.00** worth of opportunities in the **Prospect** phase of the pipeline:

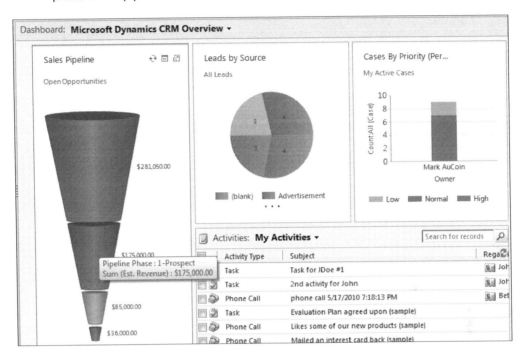

5. The tooltip will remain for a few seconds, and then it will disappear. To see information about the other segments in this chart, simply move the mouse cursor over those segments.

How it works...

Tooltips for a chart component in Dynamics CRM 2011 identify the different data series that were used to build the chart. In the **Sales Pipeline** chart example, we can see that this chart summarizes **Opportunity Estimated Revenue** data (money values), and then groups the results by the Pipeline Phase field (four different types in this example).

There's more...

Tooltips are of course not limited to just the funnel type chart (used in this example); they are present in all the chart types offered in Dynamics CRM 2011.

Tooltips for stacked bar charts

When working with a **stacked bar** chart, as in the **Cases By Priority (Per Owner)** chart in the dashboard shown in the following screenshot, the tooltips are also stacked. Compared to a normal bar chart where there will be a single tooltip for the entire bar, a stacked bar chart will contain a different tooltip for each segment of the stack.

1. Using the **Cases By Priority (Per Owner)** chart, move your mouse cursor over the first segment in the single stacked bar. You will see a tooltip showing information related to that single segment of the total bar value:

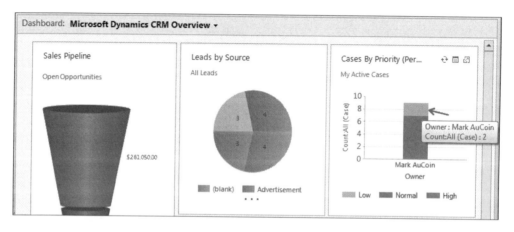

2. Next, move your mouse cursor down to another segment in the stack. You will notice that the tooltip changes to reflect data related to that segment of the chart:

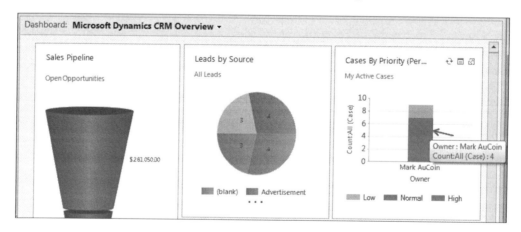

Refreshing dashboard data

The chart and list dashboard components in Dynamics CRM 2011 allow users to see live data at a glance. The dashboard data is live, but sometimes you might need to force a refresh of the data you are viewing.

Getting ready

Using Dynamics CRM 2011, navigate to the **Dashboards** section.

How to do it...

Carry out the following steps in order to complete this recipe:

1. Select the **Microsoft Dynamics CRM Overview** dashboard from the list of available dashboard items. The dashboard will refresh and build itself using live data from your Dynamics CRM system as shown in the following screenshot.

2. Once the dashboard has finished rendering, you will see all the different components such as charts and lists:

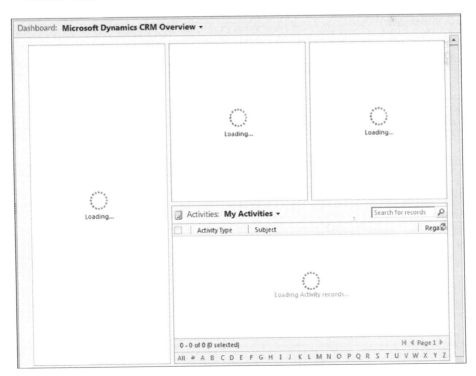

3. If data has been modified in the system, you might want to refresh a single component of the dashboard; let's say it was the **Leads by Source** chart. Move your mouse cursor over the chart and a small menu will appear with three items in it.

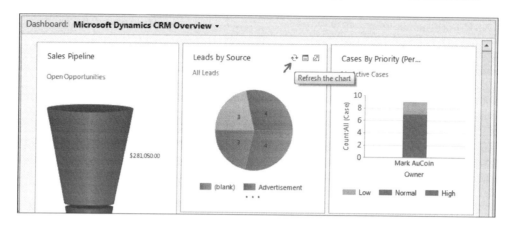

4. Click on the **Refresh the chart** option (highlighted in the preceding screenshot) and the single **Leads by Source** chart will refresh while leaving the other dashboard components in their current state, as shown in the following screenshot:

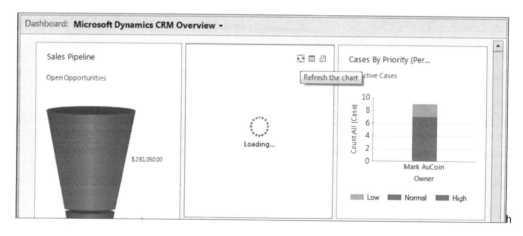

5. In order to refresh a list component on a dashboard, locate the green refresh icon, which is located at the top right-hand corner of the list component as shown in the following screenshot:

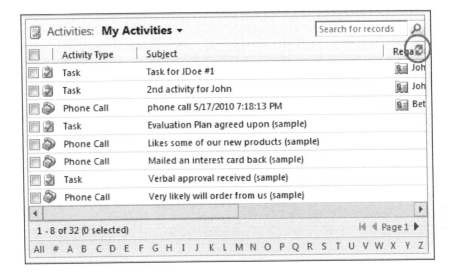

How it works...

Clicking on the **Refresh list** function instructs the Dynamics CRM 2011 system to re-query the dataset that was used to render the component. This means that any changes made to the related data since you first viewed the component will be reflected in the refreshed view.

There's more...

We will now refresh non-standard dashboard components.

Refreshing non-standard dashboard components

As we will mention in upcoming recipes, a dashboard can contain many different types of components. Some of those items will refer to external components, and as such, they may not support the refresh function. If you are unsure of how to refresh a component built outside of Dynamics CRM 2011, please contact your CRM administrator.

Drilling down into a chart

Charts are a very big part of the new dashboard features in Microsoft Dynamics CRM 2011, and one of the best features of the new chart module is the ability to drill into segments of the chart data. By drilldown, we mean the ability to filter the data and focus on a particular segment of the records being used to build the chart as a whole.

Getting ready

Using Dynamics CRM 2011, navigate to the **Dashboards** section.

How to do it...

Carry out the following steps in order to complete this recipe:

1. Select the **Microsoft Dynamics CRM Overview** dashboard from the list of available dashboards.

2. Locate the **Sales Pipeline** chart, and enlarge the chart to make it easier to work with (see the *Enlarging a chart to full screen* recipe at the beginning of this chapter):

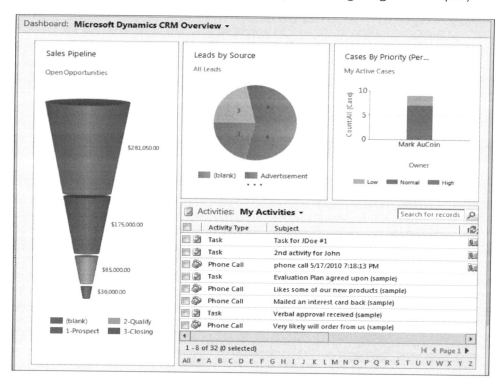

3. Click on one of the segments in the funnel chart. I would suggest the segment shown in red named **1-Prospect** as we know it has some good sample data. You will see a small pop-up menu appear, as shown in the following screenshot:

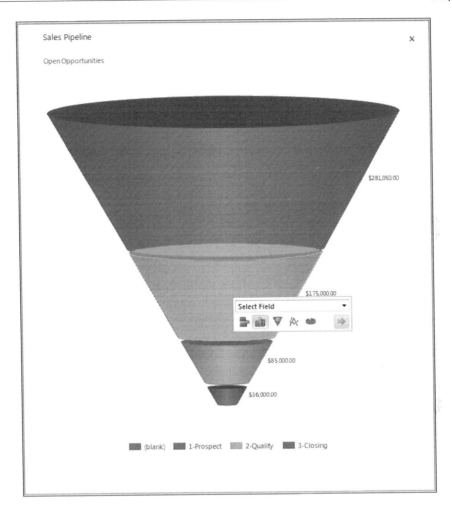

4. This menu allows you to specify how you want to drill into the segment data for this chart. Click on the **Select Field** pick list to see the field options, and select the field named **Potential Customer**.

5. Next, select the chart type that you would like to use for this new chart. Leave the default bar chart selected for now.

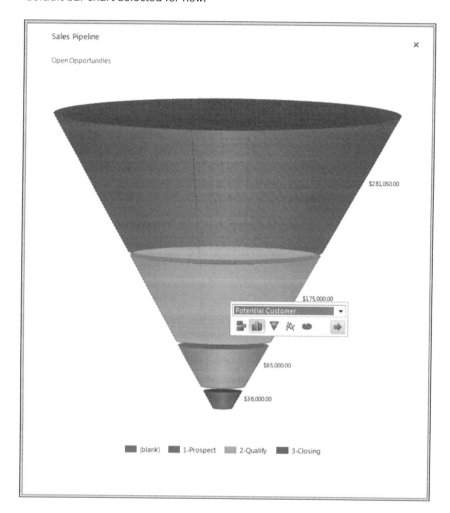

6. On the pop-up menu, click on the blue right-pointing arrow to generate the report. The resulting chart will show the open opportunities that have a pipeline phase equal to **1-Prospect**, and group that data by the **Potential Customer** field, as shown in the following screenshot:

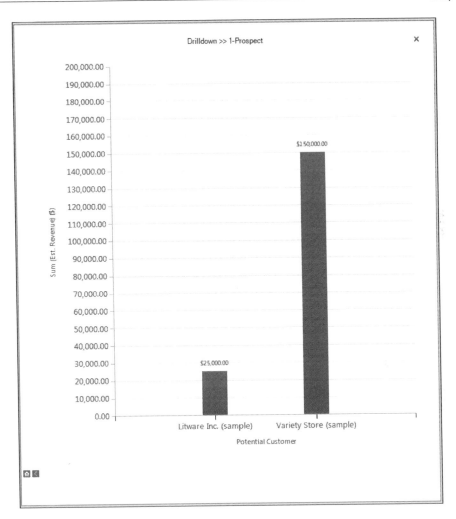

There's more...

Let's take a look at how you can get back to the original chart.

Getting back to the original chart

Once you start to drill down into the chart data, you may want to take steps back to view the original chart. There are a small blue chevron and a home icon located at the bottom left-hand corner of the new drill-down chart. Click on the chevron to move up a level in the chart data, or click on the home icon to move back to the original chart. Clicking on the **x** (shown in the following screenshot) icon will close the expanded chart and take you back to the dashboard view:

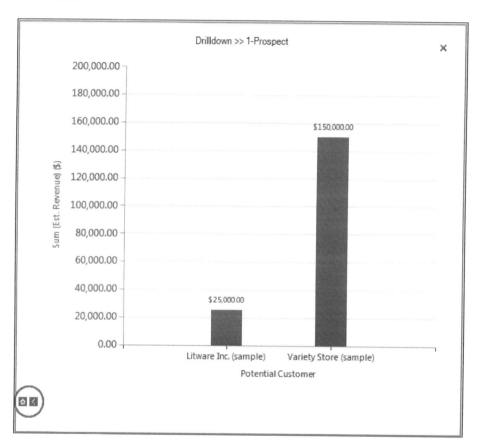

Working with inline charts and filtered records

Viewing Dynamics CRM data in charts is an excellent way to analyse data; however, sometimes you might also want to filter the raw data and have it dynamically adjust the accompanying chart. In Dynamics CRM 2011, just about every view (list) has the ability to show a related chart. This gives users the ability to start with a basic chart and list, and then filter or adjust records and see how the charts are affected.

Getting ready

Using Dynamics CRM 2011, navigate to the **Dashboards** section.

How to do it...

Carry out the following steps in order to complete this recipe:

1. Select the **Microsoft Dynamics CRM Overview** dashboard from the list of available dashboards.

2. Locate the **Sales Pipeline** chart on this dashboard. Move your mouse cursor to the upper right-hand corner of the chart and you will see a small menu appear as shown in the following screenshot:

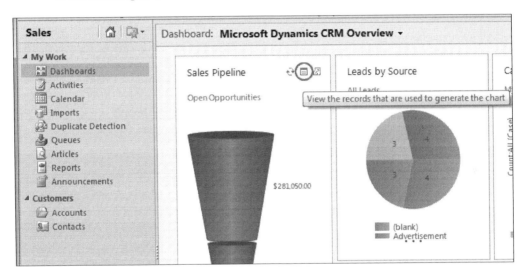

3. Click on the second menu item; the tooltip will read **View the records that are used to generate the chart**. This will launch a new browser window that contains a listing of records used to render the **Sales Pipeline** chart that happens to be shown on the **Microsoft Dynamics CRM Overview** dashboard, as shown in the following screenshot:

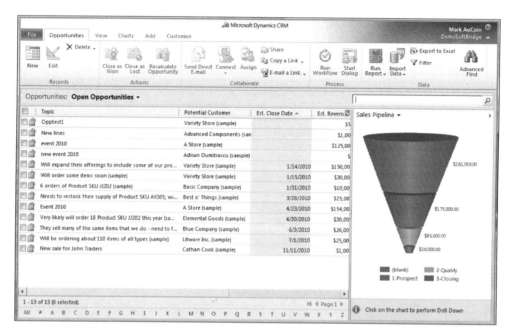

4. We want to filter this data based on the different opportunity rating values. Using the view's horizontal scrollbar, scroll all the way to the right until you see the **Rating** column heading.

5. Now, find the **Filter** command button located on the Windows Ribbon toolbar and click on it. The column headings will now have small arrows on the right side of the text indicating that a drop-down menu is now available for each column, as shown in the following screenshot:

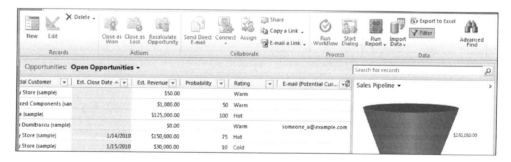

6. Click on the small drop-down arrow located in the **Rating** column's heading, as shown in the following screenshot. This will show a context menu that allows you to filter the data you see by one of this column's pick-list values:

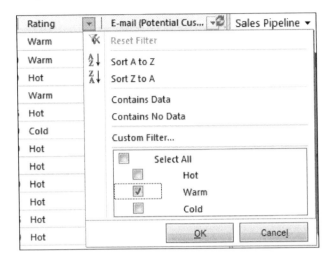

7. Check the option for the **Warm** data value and then click on the **OK** button to apply the filter rules. You may need to manually refresh the chart control; a **Refresh Chart** button will appear if you need to:

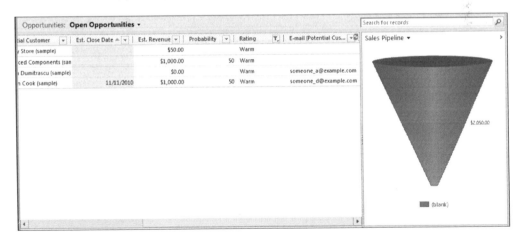

How it works...

The filter option is common across most data views in Dynamics CRM 2011. It allows you to perform quick queries and apply multiple filters to the data at the same time. The chart works from the data being shown in the list.

There's more...

We will now take a look at how we can filter data using a chart drilldown.

Filtering data by performing a chart drilldown

The chart being shown with these lists of data still supports the drill-down option (covered in the *Drilling down into a chart* recipe). When you perform a drilldown on the chart in this example, you are in effect applying a filter to the data. The data in the list located on the left side of the screen will reflect the request made when drilling into the chart.

See also

▸   The recipe named *Drilling down into a chart* in this chapter

▸   The recipe named *Filtering records in a list* in this chapter

Searching for records in a list

Along with the chart component, dashboards in Dynamics CRM 2011 can also include the list component. The list component is used to show CRM data in a tabular format. Sometimes, the list of data being presented can go over the 50 or 250 record display limit, and you will need to search for the information you are looking for.

Getting ready

Start by going to the **Dashboards** section in the Dynamics CRM 2011 **Workplace** area.

How to do it...

Carry out the following steps in order to complete this recipe:

1. Select the **Dashboards** link from the **Workplace** area.

2. If it is not currently showing, select the **Microsoft Dynamics CRM Overview** dashboard. There should be a list located near the bottom right of this dashboard with the title **My Activities**, as shown in the following screenshot:

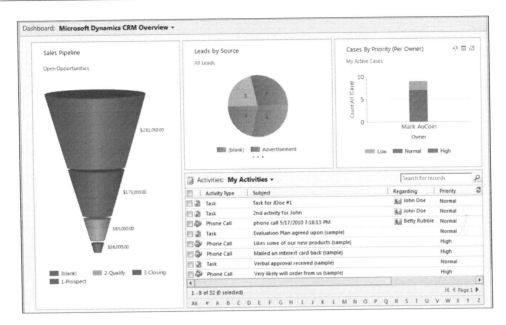

3. Move your mouse cursor over to the input box that says **Search for records**; this is the search criteria box. You will notice a tooltip appear that says **Use asterisk (*) wildcard character to search on partial text**. This means that if you don't know the complete word, or want to look for words that might be in the middle of other text, you can combine them with the asterisk (*) character to get your results.

4. In order to demonstrate this, type **like** into the search criteria box and then hit your _Enter_ key or click on the magnifying glass icon next to the input box (the related tooltip will say **Start search**). If you are still using the Dynamics CRM 2011 sample data, you should see the following two records returned in the search results. The criterion provided asks CRM for any records where the **Subject** field starts with the word **like**:

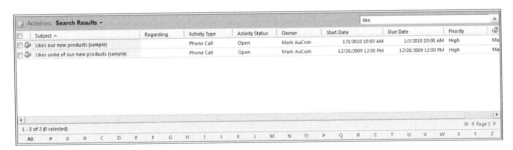

5. Next, we want to broaden the search to contain any records in the **My Activities** list where the word **like** is used in the **Subject** field. To clear the search results, you must click on the small **x** icon located where the magnifying glass was before you started the search. The related tooltip will say **Clear search**. This will return the list to the original state.

6. Type the following into the search criteria box: ***like*** and the hit your *Enter* key or click on the magnifying glass icon to start the search. If you are still using the Dynamics CRM 2011 sample data, you should now see the following three records returned in the search results. The extra record is a result of widening the search criteria by instructing to look for any records where the **Subject** field contains the word **like**:

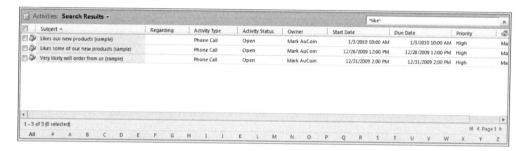

How it works...

The list component on the dashboard allows the dashboard creator to show one or more of the system views that were created earlier in the Dynamics CRM application. A view is basically a query that has predefined display columns and predefined criteria. The list used in this recipe was looking at the **My Activities** view. That view had certain display columns (**Subject, Regarding, Activity Type**, and so on) and predefined criteria (*show all CRM Activity records that I own*). It is important to note that the **My Activities** view only defined the **Subject** field to be used as a **Find Column**. The Find Column of a view is used when performing searches. So when we typed in the word **like**, it only checked for matching results using the **Subject** field values.

There's more...

Modifying and creating system views is outside the scope of this recipe, but it is important to understand this behavior if you are not getting the expected results in your list searches, and is also something to consider when designing items to be put on a dashboard.

Searching against a view with multiple Find Columns

As discussed earlier, views can be defined to have multiple Find Columns, and by design, when searching lists the comparisons can check against multiple field values. To demonstrate this, as I have the CRM Customizer security role, I modified the **Activity** entity's **Quick Find All Activities** view to include both the **Subject** field and the **Regarding** field as **Find Columns** for search results.

> ▶ If you have the appropriate security role, modify the Activity's **Quick Find All Activities** view in the same way as mentioned above, then navigate to the **Microsoft Dynamics CRM Overview** dashboard, locate the **My Activities** list and type the word ***doe*** into the search criteria box.

> ▶ Hit the *Enter* key to launch the search and get the following results that contain records where the **Subject** field contains the word **Doe**, and also records where the **Regarding** field contains the word **Doe**, as shown in the following screenshot:

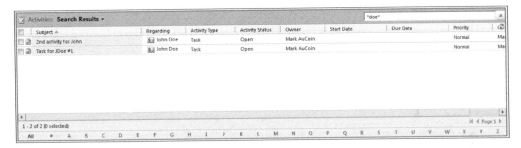

Sorting records in a list

When working with a list of mixed records displayed in a dashboard list component, you may need to **sort** that data to make it more manageable. You can sort in ascending and descending order. You can also sort by multiple column headings.

Getting ready

Start by going to the **Dashboards** section in the Dynamics CRM 2011 **Workplace** area.

How to do it...

Carry out the following steps in order to complete this recipe:

1. Select the **Dashboards** link from the **Workplace** area.

2. Select the **Microsoft Dynamics CRM Overview** dashboard. There should be a list located near the bottom right of this dashboard with the title **My Activities**. By default, this list is sorted by the **Due Date** column, as indicated by an arrow located in the column heading, as shown in the following screenshot:

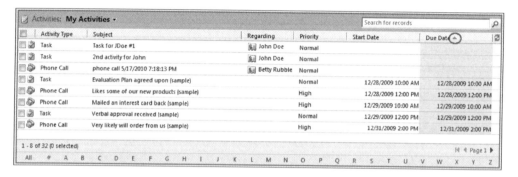

3. The arrowhead pointing up indicates that this column is being sorted in ascending order (lowest to highest). Click on the **Due Date** column heading again to change the column sorting to descending order (highest to lowest), as shown in the following screenshot:

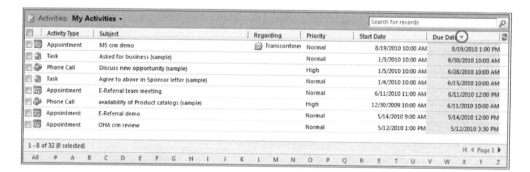

There's more...

Any column sorting that has been applied to the list component will not be remembered by the dashboard. If you leave this dashboard and come back, any sorting changes you made will be reset to the default sort.

How to sort a list by multiple columns

A list in Dynamics CRM 2011 can also be sorted by multiple columns at the same time. This is useful when trying to quickly focus on a segment of data.

▶ Click on the **Priority** column heading; this will set it up in ascending order with an upwards facing arrow in the heading, as shown in the following screenshot:

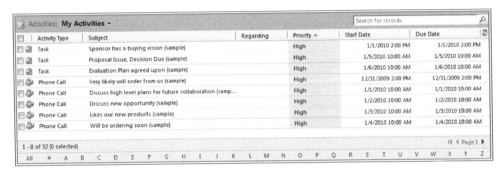

▶ Next, hold down the *Shift* key on your keyboard and click on the **Activity Type** column. Both columns now have arrows in the column headings and the list has been resorted, as shown in the following screenshot:

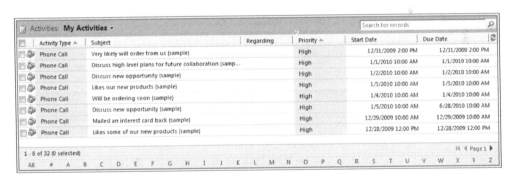

Filtering records in a list

List components in Dynamics CRM 2011 have a powerful feature named **Filtering**. This is very similar to the column filter feature available in Microsoft Excel, and just as useful when dealing with large segments of data in a list.

Getting ready

Start by going to the **Dashboards** section in the Dynamics CRM 2011 **Workplace** area.

How to do it...

Carry out the following steps in order to complete this recipe:

1. Select the **Dashboards** link from the **Workplace** area.

2. Select the **Microsoft Dynamics CRM Overview** dashboard. There should be a list located near the bottom right of this dashboard with the title **My Activities**.

3. Select that list; you will notice a light blue highlighted box that appears around the entire list component as shown in the following screenshot:

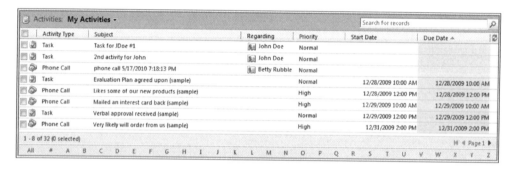

4. The ribbon (toolbar) in Dynamics CRM 2011 will change to show commands related to the list you have highlighted (**My Activities**). Click on the **Filter** button located in the **Current View** section of the ribbon as shown in the following screenshot:

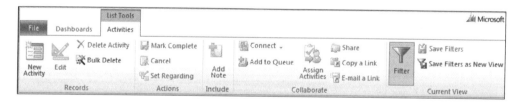

5. Once you enable filtering, each of the column headings in the list will get a small drop-down menu icon located to the right of the column heading text. Click on the drop-down menu icon for the **Priority** field to see the options available as shown in the following screenshot:

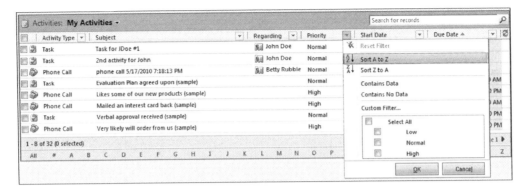

6. From the list of available options (**Low**, **Normal**, and **High**), select the item labeled **Low** and then click on the **OK** button. The list data will now be filtered to only include activities where the **Priority** value equals **Low**, as shown in the following screenshot:

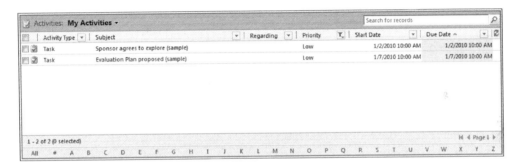

7. In order to clear the filter from the **Priority** column, click on the small filter icon located in the column heading again. The first menu item in the filter menu will be called **Reset Filter**. Click on the **Reset Filter** menu item and the **Priority** equals **Low filter** will be removed:

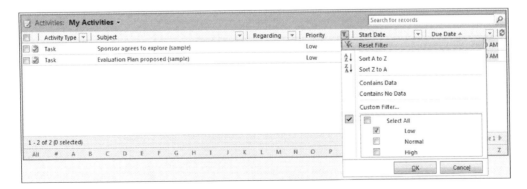

How it works...

In this recipe, we worked with the Activity's **Priority** field, and as this field was designed as an **Option Set** field (a field that contains a series of options that are displayed in a pick-list control), the filter menu being displayed included the list of options available to the user when they see this field on a data form. The user can pick from a list of valid items instead of trying to remember what to type in when building the filter condition.

There's more...

Filters applied to the list component are not stored with the dashboard. If you leave this dashboard and come back, the filters will be cleared. When filtering is enabled on a list, there is a default set of actions that can be executed on each column regardless of the data type. The following screenshot shows the various actions that can be executed on a column:

- ▸ **Sort A to Z** applies an ascending search order to the column data.
- ▸ **Sort Z to A** applies a descending search order to the column data.
- ▸ **Contains Data** only shows records where there is data in this column.
- ▸ **Contains No Data** shows records where there is no data in this column.
- ▸ **Custom Filter** allows the user to build an **AND/OR** condition for this column. The options available are the same as those seen in the expanded filter menu, but you can specify multiple conditions along with a more complex **OR** condition when needed:

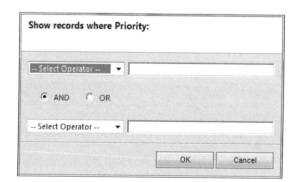

Custom filtering on a text column

When performing a filter on a **text** column, you can use the default options (listed earlier in this recipe) or you can use the **Custom Filter** option.

1. Turn on filtering and open the filter options located to the right of the column text for the **Subject** column.

2. Select the **Custom Filter** option.

3. In the first **Select Operator** pick list, select the **Contains** option and type the word **like** in the criteria field.

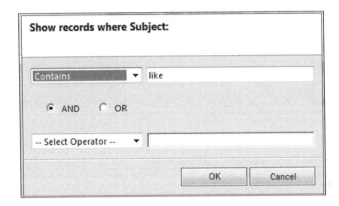

4. Click on the **OK** button to see your results. They should show all records where the word **like** was somewhere in the **Subject** field:

Filtering on a Lookup type column

If you are filtering on a Lookup type column (a field that creates a link to another record in the system), you will have the **Filter by specific Regarding** option, which will let you specify exactly which related records to include in the filter condition.

1. Turn on filtering and open the filter options menu for the **Regarding** column as shown in the following screenshot:

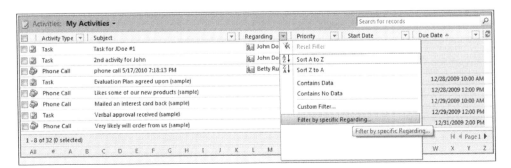

2. Click on the **Filter by specific Regarding** menu item. You will be presented with a **Look Up Records** dialog. Locate the **John Doe** contact record and add it to the **Selected records** list. Click on the **OK** button as shown in the following screenshot:

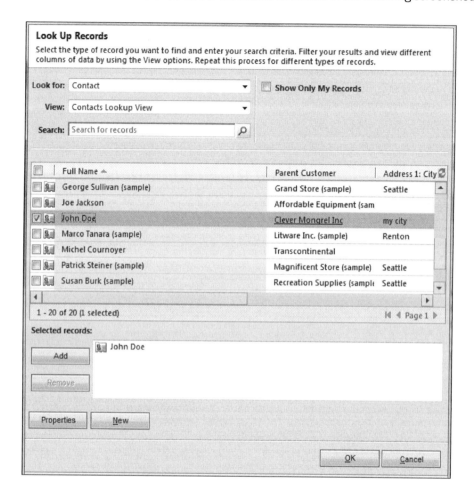

3. Your list will only contain Activity records that are regarding **John Doe**.

Filtering on a Date column

When filtering on a Date column there are many options available. All of these options are date specific and very flexible.

▶ Turn on the filtering and open the filter options menu for the **Start Date** column as shown in the following screenshot:

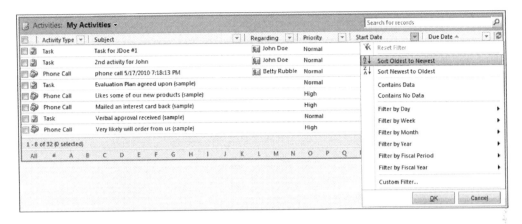

> ► Click on the **Filter by Year** menu item, and then on the **Last Year** item. Click on the **OK** button to apply the changes, as shown in the following screenshot:

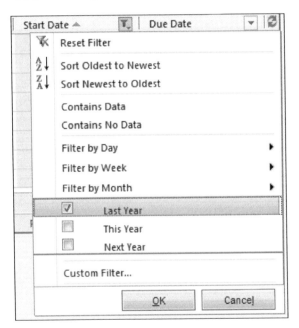

> ► The data list will now contain records where the **Start Date** value falls within last year only. This new filter condition is being applied on top of the view's base filter, which is set up to show My Activities. It appends to the search parameters, but does not remove the original parameters.

Changing the view for a dashboard list

When looking at a list of records on a dashboard, you might have the option of changing the view being presented in the list component. The option to select a different view is decided by the dashboard designer.

Getting ready

Start by going to the **Dashboards** section in the Dynamics CRM 2011 **Workplace** area.

How to do it...

Carry out the following steps in order to complete this recipe:

1. Select the **Dashboards** link from the **Workplace** area.

2. Highlight the **My Activities** list component. If the view being displayed can be changed, there will be a small drop-down menu icon next to the title of the view as shown in the following screenshot:

3. Clicking on this icon will display a list of available views to which you can switch:

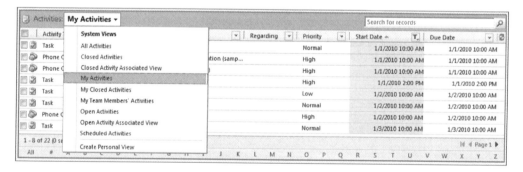

4. Select the **My Closed Activities** item from the list of views , as shown in the following screenshot. This will cause the list component to switch the view and load the requested data:

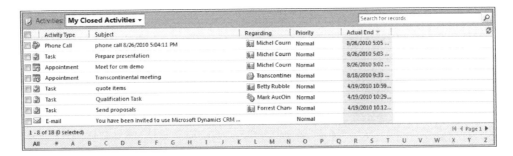

There's more...

If the user changes the selected view on a list component, this will not override the default view setting. If you leave this dashboard and come back, you would be shown the default view.

3
Creating a Dashboard

In this chapter, we will cover:

- ▶ Creating a user dashboard
- ▶ Creating a system dashboard
- ▶ Changing the layout of your dashboard
- ▶ Adding a chart to your dashboard
- ▶ Editing a chart on your dashboard
- ▶ Adding a list to a dashboard
- ▶ Editing a list on a dashboard

Introduction

The previous chapters focused on exploring and interacting with the dashboards that come with Dynamics CRM 2011. This chapter will introduce you to creating your own personal dashboard that contains charts that you will pick.

Creating a user dashboard

This recipe will explain the steps required to create your first **user dashboard**.

Getting ready

Navigate to the **Dashboards** section in the Dynamics CRM 2011 **Workplace** area.

How to do it...

Carry out the following steps in order to complete this recipe:

1. Select the **Dashboards** link from the **Workplace** area. The default dashboard will be displayed.

2. The **Dashboards** ribbon should also be displayed along the top of the screen. Click on the **New** button to start the process, as shown in the following screenshot:

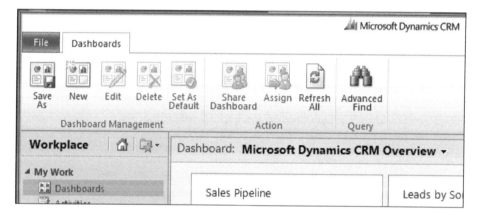

3. The **Select Dashboard Layout** dialog will appear. It contains a listing of the six default layouts available when creating a new dashboard. For this recipe, select the **3-Column Regular Dashboard** layout, and then click on the **Create** button, as shown in the following screenshot:

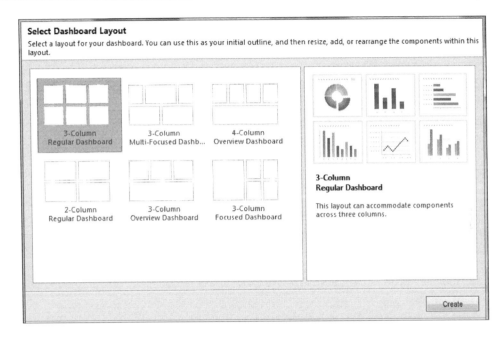

4. The dashboard designer screen will now appear. Provide the required **Name** value for your new dashboard and hit the **Save and Close** button.

5. Once the dashboard editor window has closed, you will be back at the **Dashboards** section in Dynamics CRM 2011, and you will see your new (albeit empty) dashboard. In this example, it was named **My First Dashboard**, as shown in the following screenshot:

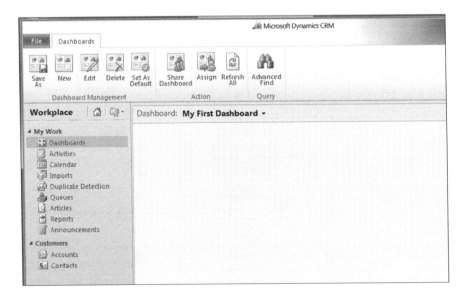

6. Referring back to the **Dashboards** ribbon again, click on the **Edit** button to open the dashboard editor window for your new dashboard.

How it works...

Rather than creating physical files for each dashboard, the dashboard editor stores an XML record containing the layout of the dashboard within the Dynamics CRM database. This record is retrieved by the system and rendered when a user requests a dashboard to be displayed.

There's more...

Let's explore the six different layouts.

When you click on the **New** button from the **Dashboards** ribbon, a **Select Dashboard Layout** screen appears that contains the six default layouts to help you get started. This section shows examples of how to use these layouts and explains how each of the layout types might be used.

3-Column Regular Dashboard

This layout provides placeholders for six components. That is, two rows of three columns in a grid format. There is one section container on this dashboard, so that you can provide a subtitle if needed. The following screenshot shows an example:

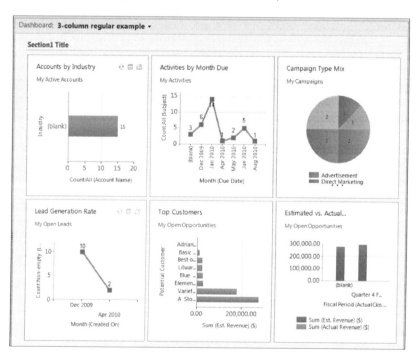

3-Column Multi-Focused Dashboard

This layout provides space for five components. The component placeholders are of different sizes, and have been designed that way to draw the attention (focus) of the user to a couple of components when first viewed. There is one section container on this dashboard, so that you can provide a subtitle if needed. The following screenshot shows an example:

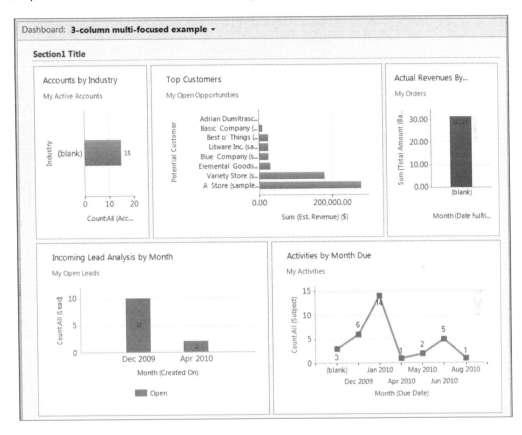

4-Column Overview Dashboard

This layout has two rows by default. The first row has four columns, which can be used to display charts and other components. The second row has one wide column, which is suitable for showing a list control, a wide chart, or an IFrame component. There are two collapsible tabs, each with one section container so that you can provide a subtitle if needed. The following screenshot shows an example:

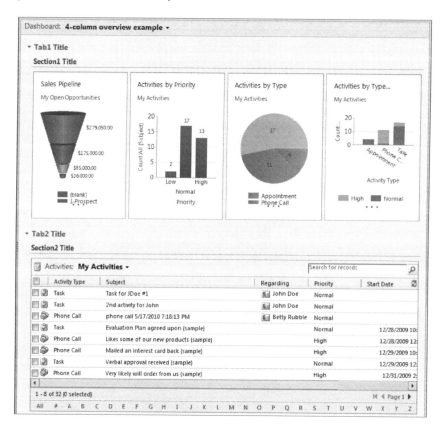

2-Column Regular Dashboard

This layout provides placeholders for four components. That is, two rows of two columns in a grid format. There is one section container on this dashboard, so that you can provide a subtitle if needed. The following screenshot shows an example:

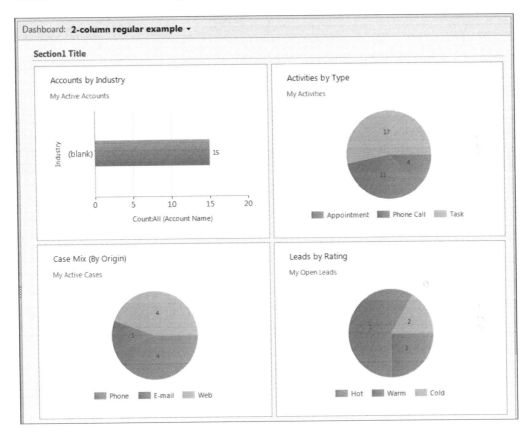

3-Column Overview Dashboard

This layout has two rows by default. The first row has three columns and can be used to display any smaller components. The second row has one large column, which is suitable for showing wide list controls, charts, and IFrames. There are two collapsible tabs, each with one section container so that you can provide a subtitle if needed. The following screenshot shows an example:

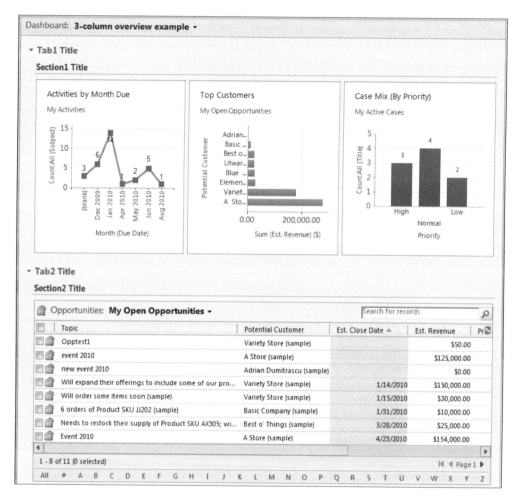

3-Column Focused Dashboard

This layout contains three main columns to display components; however, the first column can be used to draw focus to a specific component that might require more vertical space. There is one section container on this dashboard, so that you can provide a subtitle if needed. The following screenshot shows an example:

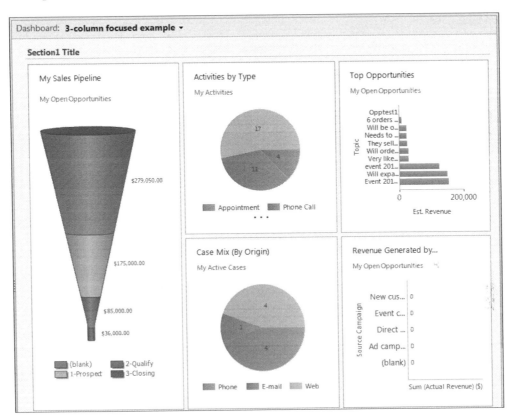

Creating a system dashboard

The **system dashboards** are intended to be viewed by all users of Dynamics CRM. These dashboards are created and managed by users with the **System Customizer** or **System Administrator** security roles.

Getting ready

Creating a system dashboard requires you to navigate to the **Customization** section in the Dynamics CRM 2011 **Settings** area.

How to do it...

Carry out the following steps in order to complete this recipe:

1. From the **Customization** section, click on the **Customize the System** link, as shown in the following screenshot:

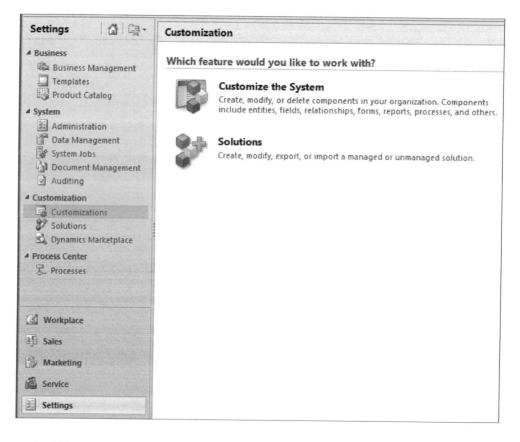

2. This will launch the **Solution Editor** dialog showing the **Default Solution** for Dynamics CRM 2011. Click on the **Dashboards** link located in the left-hand navigation section, as shown in the following screenshot:

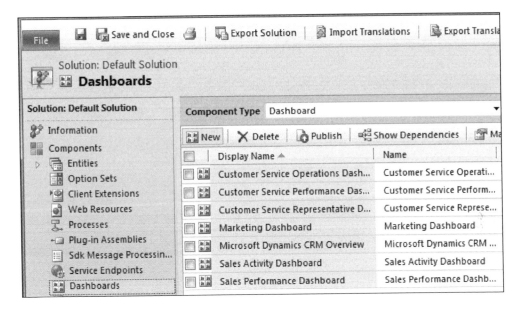

3. A listing of the existing system dashboards will be shown. Clicking on the **New** button will start the process of creating a dashboard. These steps are covered in more detail in the *Creating a user dashboard* recipe.

There's more...

Changes and additions made to system-wide components (such as system dashboards) in Dynamics CRM need to be published in order for the users to receive those changes.

Publishing the system dashboard

One of the big differences between creating a system dashboard and a user dashboard is that a system dashboard requires you to **publish** the changes before they can be seen by the Dynamics CRM users.

For this example, I created a new system dashboard named **Accounts Overview Dashboard**. From the solution explorer window's **Dashboards** list, I selected the new system dashboard and clicked on the **Publish** button on the toolbar, as shown in the following screenshot:

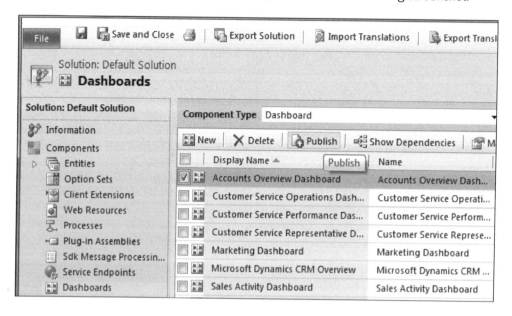

After the publishing is completed, the new system dashboard (or changes made to an existing system dashboard) will be committed and available to other users of the Dynamics CRM system.

Changing the layout of your dashboard

When creating a new dashboard, you are prompted to select a default layout; this was outlined earlier in the *Creating a user dashboard* recipe. However, you might need to design a dashboard that requires a different layout than those provided in the six default layouts. In order to handle this, Dynamics CRM 2011 lets the dashboard editor modify portions of the layout to better accommodate your needs.

Getting ready

Navigate to the **Dashboards** section in the Dynamics CRM 2011 **Workplace** area.

How to do it...

Carry out the following steps in order to complete this recipe:

1. Select the **Dashboards** link from the **Workplace** area.

2. Select the same personal dashboard that we created in the first recipe of this chapter (*Creating a user dashboard*).

3. From the **Dashboards** menu in the Dynamics CRM 2011 ribbon, click on the **Edit** button, as highlighted in the following screenshot:

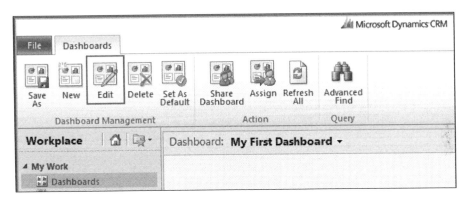

4. The dashboard editor screen will open, and your dashboard will be in the edit mode. By using the mouse select the first component placeholder in the first row, on the left. When you select a dashboard component, it will become highlighted with a blue border as seen in the following screenshot:

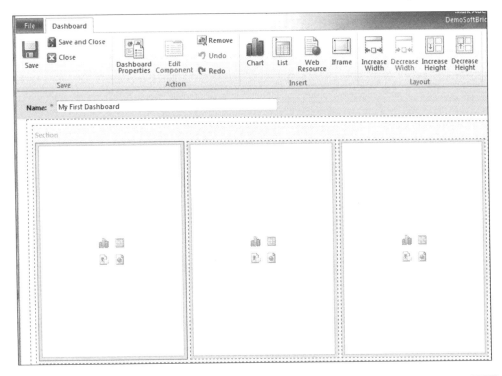

5. Remove the selected component placeholder by clicking on the **Remove** button located in the **Dashboard** ribbon toolbar, as shown in the following screenshot:

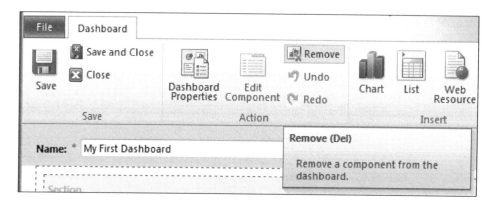

6. Once the item has been removed, you will notice that the component placeholder sitting below it has moved up to fill in the empty space. By default, the top section of a dashboard cannot be blank. Make sure that the first item on the left side is still selected, as shown in the following screenshot:

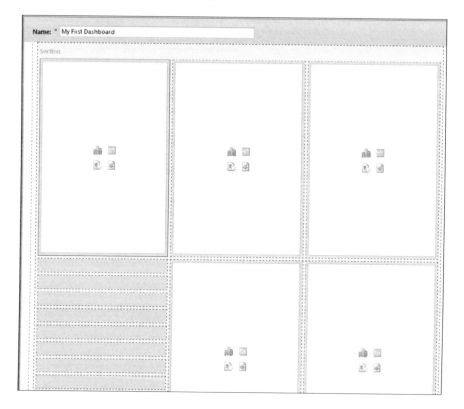

7. Locate the **Increase Height** button in the dashboard editor's ribbon toolbar. Click on this button four times until the selected component placeholder becomes two rows tall:

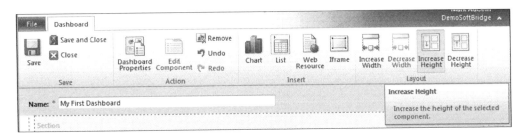

8. Next, select the component placeholder located in the bottom right of the dashboard, as highlighted in the following screenshot:

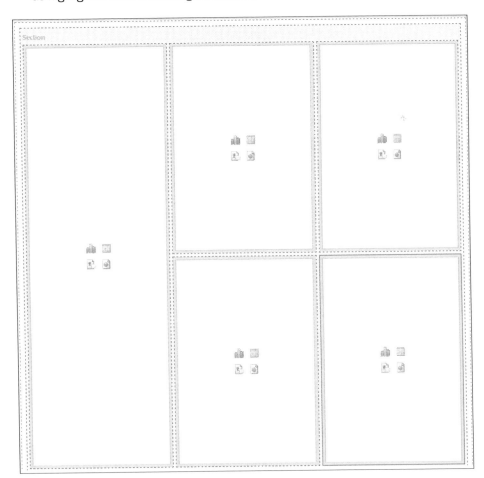

9. Remove the selected component placeholder by clicking on the **Remove** button in the **Dashboard** ribbon toolbar.

10. Select the only remaining small component placeholder in the bottom row.

11. Locate the **Increase Width** button in the **Dashboard** toolbar ribbon. Click on the **Increase Width** button once and the selected component placeholder will fill the available horizontal space in the dashboard:

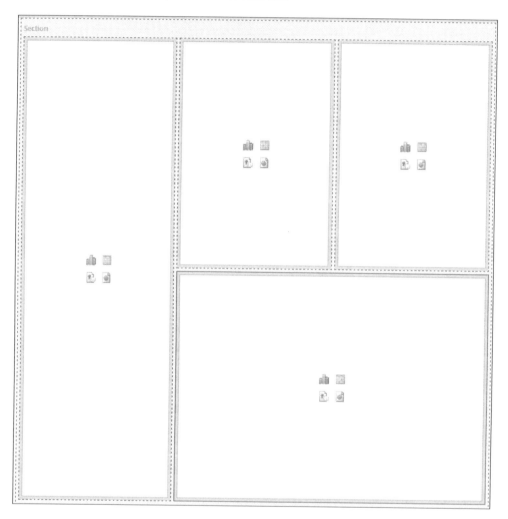

12. Click on the **Save** button in the **Dashboard** ribbon toolbar to save your custom layout configuration, as shown in the following screenshot:

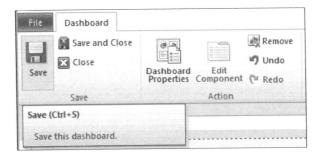

There's more...

When editing a dashboard, the components can be moved by using a drag-and-drop similar to moving files around your desktop. There will be a small red highlight that shows you where the dragged item will be dropped.

Adding a chart to your dashboard

Earlier in this chapter there were recipes that showed how to create a dashboard and modify the layout of a dashboard. This recipe will build on that dashboard by adding a Dynamics CRM Chart component to view some data.

Getting ready

Navigate to the **Dashboards** section in the Dynamics CRM 2011 **Workplace** area.

How to do it...

Carry out the following steps in order to complete this recipe:

1. Select the **Dashboards** link from the **Workplace** area.

2. Select the same personal dashboard we created in the first recipe (*Creating a user dashboard*) of this chapter.

3. From the **Dashboards** menu in the Dynamics CRM 2011 ribbon, click on the **Edit** button, as highlighted in the following screenshot:

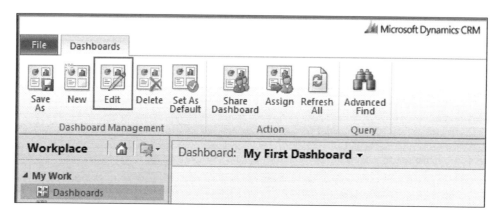

4. The dashboard editor screen will open, and your dashboard will be in edit mode. By using the mouse, click on the chart icon located in the first component placeholder, as highlighted in the following screenshot:

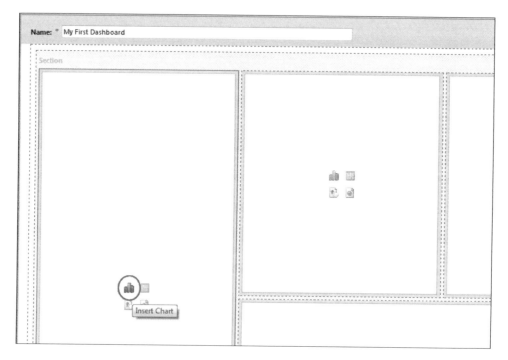

5. The **Component Designer** window will appear and this is where you can select the chart to be added to the dashboard. Change the **Record Type** field to **Opportunity**.

6. Change the **View** field to **My Open Opportunities**.

7. Change the **Chart** field to **Sales Pipeline.** The dialog box should look similar to the following screenshot:

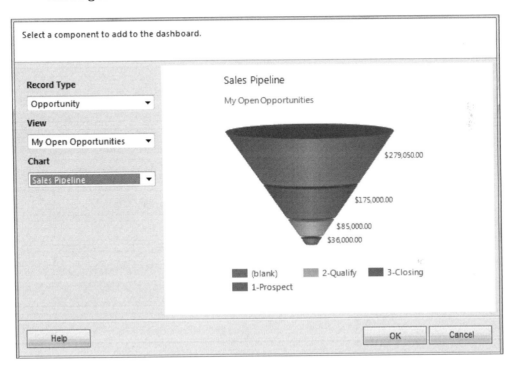

8. Click on the **OK** button to have this chart added to the dashboard.

9. Back on the dashboard, click on the **Save and Close** button in the toolbar.

10. This will take you back to your dashboard in the **Workplace** section. The**Sales Pipeline** funnel chart will be displayed on the custom dashboard, as shown in the following screenshot:

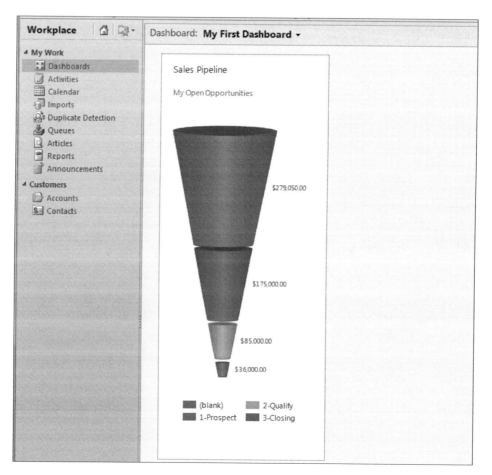

There's more...

You can add multiple charts to the dashboard by selecting one of the other empty component placeholders and following the same steps to select the proper chart, list, IFrame, or WebResource component.

Where did the charts come from?

When adding a new chart to a dashboard, the list of available charts that appears in the **Component Designer** includes those that have already been created as a part of the standard Microsoft Dynamics CRM solution along with custom charts that may have been created by the CRM Administrators for your system.

Editing a chart on your dashboard

In the previous recipe, we added a new chart to a personal dashboard. This recipe will cover editing the different settings that are available for displaying a chart on a dashboard.

Getting ready

Navigate to the **Dashboards** section in the Dynamics CRM 2011 **Workplace** area.

How to do it...

Carry out the following steps in order to complete this recipe:

1. Select the **Dashboards** link from the **Workplace** area.

2. Select the same personal dashboard that we created earlier in this chapter in the first recipe (*Creating a user dashboard*).

3. From the **Dashboards** menu in the Dynamics CRM 2011 ribbon, click on the **Edit** button, as highlighted in the following screenshot:

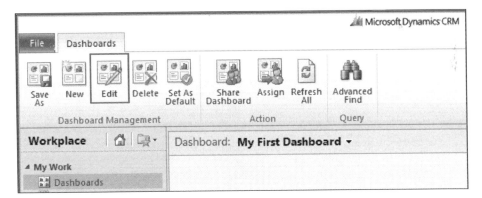

4. The dashboard editor screen will open, and your dashboard will be in edit mode. Select the **Sales Pipeline** chart and click on the **Edit Component** button in the ribbon toolbar, as shown in the following screenshot:

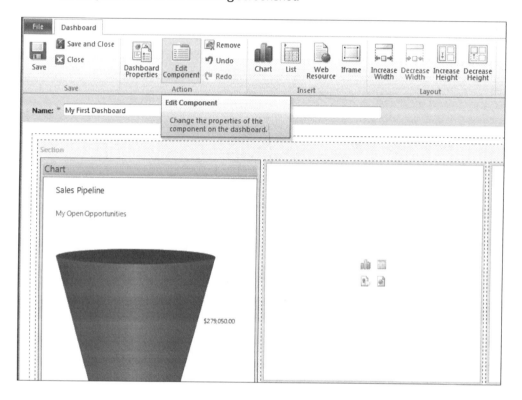

5. The **List or Chart Properties** dialog will appear. This dialog is different from the **Component Designer** window that you saw when we added a chart to this dashboard earlier in the *Adding a chart to your dashboard* recipe. The following screenshot and sections will explain the different settings in detail:

List or Chart Properties
Modify the List or Chart properties.

Name
Specify a unique name.

Name * | Component2f8569b |

Name

Label * | Opportunity |

☐ Display label on the Dashboard

Data Source
Specify the primary data source for this list or chart.

Records | All Record Types   ▼ |
Entity | Opportunities   ▼ |
Default View | My Open Opportunities   ▼ |

Additional Options

☐   Display Search Box

☐   Display Index

View Selector | Off   ▼ |

My Open Opportunities
Open Opportunities
Opportunities Closing Next Month
Opportunities Opened Last Week

Chart Options

Default Chart | Sales Pipeline   ▼ |

☑   Show Chart Only

☐   Display Chart Selection

| Help | | OK | | Cancel |

There's more...

When editing a chart control in the dashboard editor, there are many options that can be configured by the user. This section will review each of those options.

Changing the name or label for the chart

The **Name** field contains a unique ID that is used to identify each chart component within the dashboard. This value is internal, and will not be shown when the chart is displayed.

The **Label** field can be used to display a title for the chart when used on a dashboard. In order to show the label, provide a descriptive value and select the **Display label on the Dashboard** checkbox. The **Label** property can only be modified when the chart or list components—that is the **View Selector** option—is not set to **Off**. Otherwise, the label value is set to the name of the view that is providing the data records:

Changing the data source for the chart

The data that is gathered and used to generate the chart is based on the settings identified in the **Data Source** section of the **List or Chart Properties** window. Two of the following three fields in this section can be configured:

- ▶ **Records**: This field will be set to **All Record Types**. The value does not need to be changed when working with chart components.

- ▶ **Entity**: This field lets you change the entity type for this chart component. Changing this value affects the list of available views in the **Default View** field. In our example, the **Entity** field is set to **Opportunities**, which means the chart will show **Opportunity** data in the visualization.

- ▶ **Default View**: This field lists the available data views for the entity type that was selected in the **Entity** field. The selected view will provide the data needed to generate the chart visualization.

These options are depicted in the following screenshot:

Changing the additional options

The **Additional Options** section has a few settings that are only applicable when viewing a list and chart combination (the left-hand side of the component would show a list of data, while the right-hand side would show the chart visualization). In this example, we are only dealing with a single chart component, therefore, the **Display Search Box** and **Display Index** settings are not applicable and will be disabled.

The **View Selector** determines if the dashboard user can change the view being used to provide data for the selected chart. For example, a user could start with the chart using a view of all *active records*, and then switch the chart view to look at *inactive records* for comparison:

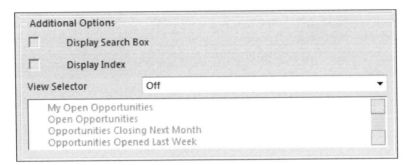

Changing the chart being displayed

The **Chart Options** section identifies the default chart being shown for the component. The **Default Chart** field provides a list of the available charts that you can set as the default chart. The list of available charts is dependent on the value of the **Entity** field located in the **Data Source** section of this window.

The **Show Chart Only** option lets you decide if the user sees only a chart component or a mix of a chart and associated data view.

The **Display Chart Selection** option allows the dashboard user to change the **Default Chart** at runtime. If the user changes the chart at runtime, those changes will not be saved with the dashboard. Every time the dashboard is visited, the original **Default Chart** is shown:

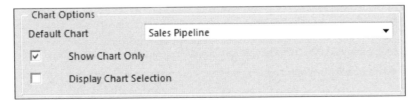

Adding a list to a dashboard

Lists are valuable tools when viewing data. In *Chapter 2, Interacting with Dashboards*, we covered how users can search, sort, and filter data in a list. This recipe will show you how to add new list to a user dashboard.

Getting ready

Navigate to the **Dashboards** section in the Dynamics CRM 2011 **Workplace** area.

How to do it...

Carry out the following steps in order to complete this recipe:

1. Select the **Dashboards** link from the **Workplace** area.

2. Select the same personal dashboard we created in the first recipe (*Creating a user dashboard*).

3. From the **Dashboards** menu in the Dynamics CRM 2011 ribbon, click on the **Edit** button, as highlighted in the following screenshot:

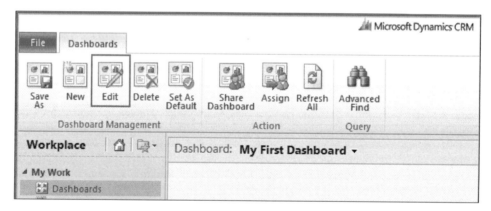

4. The dashboard editor screen will open, and your dashboard will be in edit mode. In order to place a list into an existing placeholder spot, use the mouse, and click on the list icon located in the large bottom-right component placeholder, as highlighted in the following screenshot:

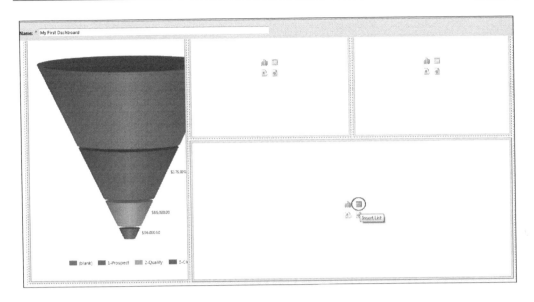

5. The **Component Designer** window will appear and this is where you select the list to be added to the dashboard. Leave the **Record Type** setting as **Accounts**.

6. Leave the **View** setting as **My Active Accounts**. The dialog will now look similar to the following screenshot:

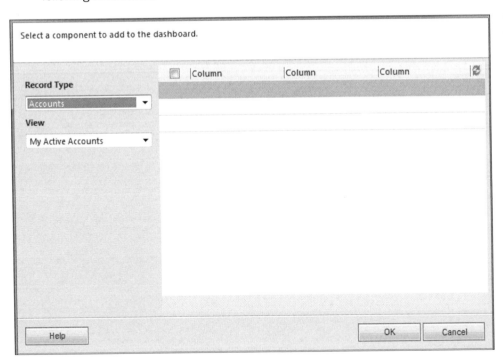

7. Click on the **OK** button to add this list to the dashboard.

8. Back on the dashboard, click on the **Save and Close** button in the toolbar.

9. This will take you back to your dashboard in the **Workplace** section. The **My Active Accounts** view will be displayed in a list on the dashboard, as shown in the following screenshot:

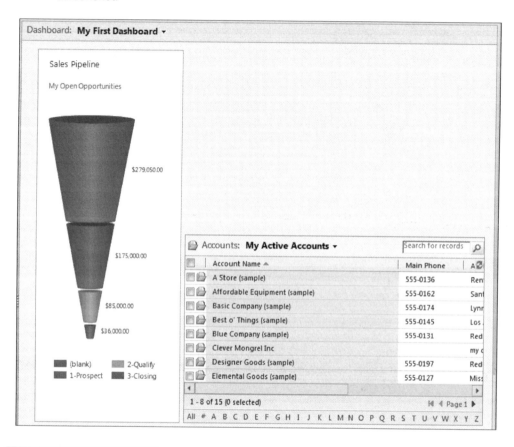

How it works...

The list component displays an existing CRM data view. In previous versions of Dynamics CRM, before Dashboards were available, developers would create ASP.NET pages that used IFrames containing a link to an existing CRM view. This complexity has been replaced with the new standard feature.

There's more...

You can add multiple lists to the dashboard by selecting one of the other empty component placeholders and following the same steps to select the proper list.

Where did the views come from?

When adding a new list to a dashboard, the available views that appear in the **Component Designer** have already been created as part of the standard Microsoft Dynamics CRM solution. Any new user views created by you or system views created by the CRM Administrators will also be available.

Editing a list on a dashboard

In the previous recipe, we added a new list to a user dashboard. This recipe will review the different settings that are available for displaying a list on a dashboard.

Getting ready

Navigate to the **Dashboards** section in the Dynamics CRM 2011 **Workplace** area.

How to do it...

Carry out the following steps in order to complete this recipe:

1. Select the **Dashboards** link from the **Workplace** area.
2. Select the same personal dashboard we created in the first recipe (*Creating a user dashboard*).

3. From the **Dashboards** menu in the Dynamics CRM 2011 ribbon, click on the **Edit** button, as highlighted in the following screenshot:

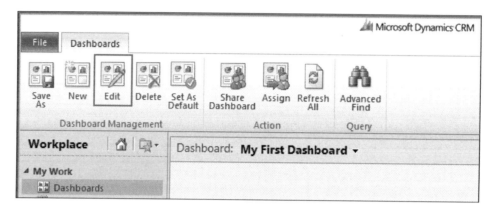

4. The dashboard editor screen will open, and your dashboard will be in the edit mode. Select the **My Active Accounts** list component and click on the **Edit Component** button in the ribbon toolbar, as shown in the following screenshot:

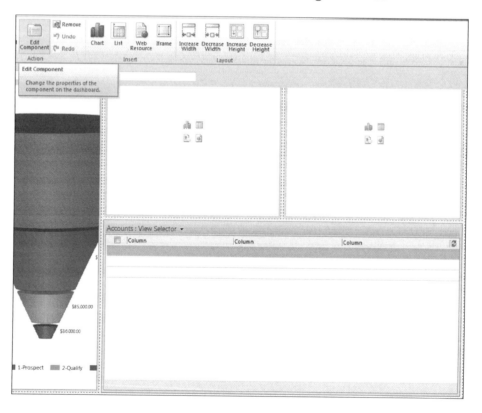

5. The **List or Chart Properties** dialog will appear. This dialog is different from the **Component Designer** window that you saw when we added a list to this dashboard earlier in the *Adding a list to your dashboard* recipe. The following screenshot and sections will explain the different settings in detail:

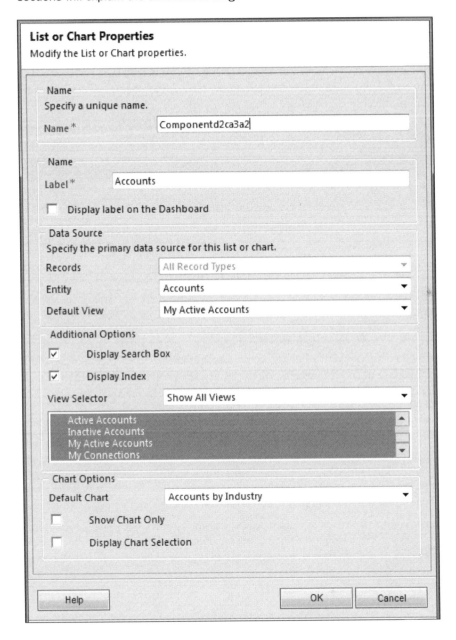

There's more...

There are many different properties available when editing a dashboard component. The following sections will go into each of these items in more detail.

Changing the name or label for the list

The **Name** field contains a unique ID that is used to identify each chart component. The ID value is for internal use by the dashboard to support features, such as drilldowns and full-screen zooms. The system will suggest an auto-generated value, but you can override this with a valid value as well. The **Label** field can be used to display a title for the list when used on a dashboard. In order to show the label, provide a descriptive value and select the **Display label on the Dashboard** checkbox, as shown in the following screenshot:

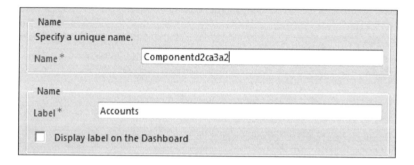

Changing the data source for the list

The data that is shown in the list is based on the settings identified in the **Data Source** section of the **List or Chart Properties** window. Any two of the three fields in this section can be configured. These fields are explained as follows:

- **Records**: This field will be set to **All Record Types**. The value does not need to be changed when working with a list component on a dashboard.

- **Entity**: This field lets you change the entity type for this list component. Changing this value affects the list of available views in the **Default View** field. In our example, the **Entity** field is set to **Accounts**, as shown in the following screenshot, which means the list will show account data.

- **Default View**: This field lists the available data views for the entity type that was selected in the **Entity** field. The selected view will provide the data and column layouts shown in the list component on the dashboard.

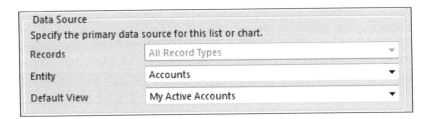

Changing the additional options

The **Additional Options** section has settings that control how the user can interact with or adjust the list component once it is on the dashboard.

The **Display Search Box** option controls whether the user can interact with a search box for this list component's data records.

Checking the **Display Index** option will display an alphabetical index (#, A-Z) that lets the user jump to records starting with the selected index character.

The **View Selector** drop-down determines if the end user can change the view currently being shown in the list component. If the option is **Off**, then the user cannot select a different view. The other two options are **Show All Views** and **Show Selected Views**, which lets you control the access, as shown in the following screenshot:

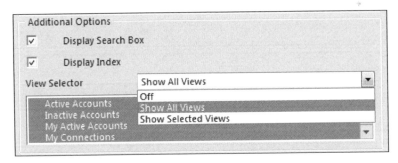

Changing the chart options

The **Chart Options** section specifies the default chart that should be displayed along with this list component. The **Default Chart** field provides a list of related charts that you can select from. The list of charts is dependent on the value of the **Entity** field located in the **Data Source** section of this window.

The **Show Chart Only** option lets you replace the list component with chart visualizations, basically the same effect as adding a chart by itself.

The **Display Chart Selection** option allows the user to change the chart being displayed alongside the list during runtime. If the user changes the chart selection, those changes will not be saved with the dashboard. Every time the dashboard is visited, the list component will show the original **Default Chart** as its companion:

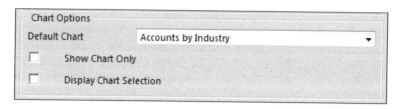

4
Sharing and Assigning Dashboards

In this chapter, we will cover:

- ► Locating the user dashboards
- ► Sharing a user dashboard
- ► Assigning a user dashboard
- ► Copying an existing dashboard

Introduction

User dashboards in Dynamics CRM 2011 are created and managed by the end user. Managing a user dashboard includes the ability to **Share** or **Assign** the dashboard with other CRM users and/or teams.

Locating the user dashboards

When viewing the list of available dashboards, the user dashboards are listed separately from the system dashboards. This is done to help the user quickly identify the set of dashboards that they have either created or have been granted access to through the sharing and assigning technique.

Getting ready

Navigate to the **Dashboards** section in the Dynamics CRM 2011 **Workplace** area.

How to do it...

Carry out the following steps in order to complete this recipe:

1. Select the **Dashboards** link from the **Workplace** area and click on the drop-down list of available dashboards, as shown in the following screenshot:

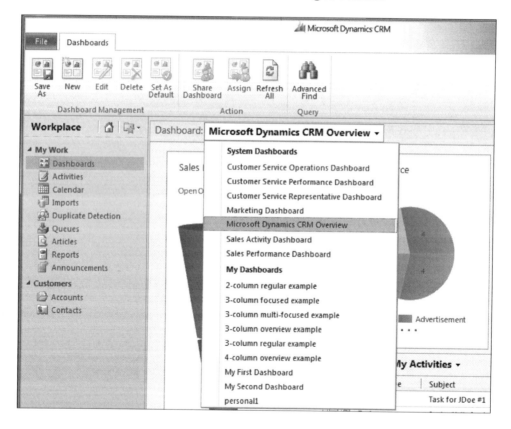

2. The collection of user dashboards will be listed under the **My Dashboards** section in this list. Select one of the user dashboards that you created in the earlier chapters, as shown in the following screenshot:

Microsoft Dynamics CRM Overview ▾

System Dashboards

Customer Service Operations Dashboard

Customer Service Performance Dashboard

Customer Service Representative Dashboard

Marketing Dashboard

Microsoft Dynamics CRM Overview

Sales Activity Dashboard

Sales Performance Dashboard

My Dashboards

2-column regular example

3-column focused example

3-column multi-focused example

3-column overview example

3-column regular example

4-column overview example

My First Dashboard

My Second Dashboard

personal1

How it works...

When you create a new user dashboard, or one is assigned to you, it will appear in the **My Dashboards** list. Dynamics CRM maintains a list of available user dashboards based on your user account's read privileges.

There's more...

Dynamics CRM allows for the creation of both user and system dashboards. The following section identifies the key differences between the two types.

The difference between user and system dashboards

Dynamics CRM supports two different types of dashboards:

▶ **User dashboards** are created and owned by an individual CRM user. User dashboards can be assigned and shared between users and teams in Dynamics CRM. When the owner makes changes to a user dashboard, those changes are available as soon as the dashboard is saved. User dashboards are generally created from the **Dashboards** section of the **Workplace** area in Dynamics CRM.

▶ **System Dashboards** are dashboards that are created by the CRM Administrator or system customizer in the systems customization area and are viewable by the entire organization. System dashboards cannot be assigned, shared, or restricted from individual users or teams within Dynamics CRM. When the CRM Administrator makes changes to a system dashboard, these changes are not available to the general users until they are published as part of the overall solution. System dashboards are created in the **Customization** section as part of the Default Solution or custom Solution Packages as part of a project.

Sharing a user dashboard

Creating your own dashboard is an excellent way to personalize the Dynamics CRM application by letting you organize the components in a way that suits your needs. **Sharing** the user dashboard allows other CRM users to access it while ensuring that you still retain ownership of that dashboard.

Getting ready

This recipe assumes that there is more than just one user account in your Dynamics CRM system. Navigate to the **Dashboards** section in the Dynamics CRM 2011 **Workplace** area.

How to do it...

Carry out the following steps:

1. Select the **Dashboards** link from the **Workplace** area and click on the drop-down list of available dashboards, as shown in the following screenshot:

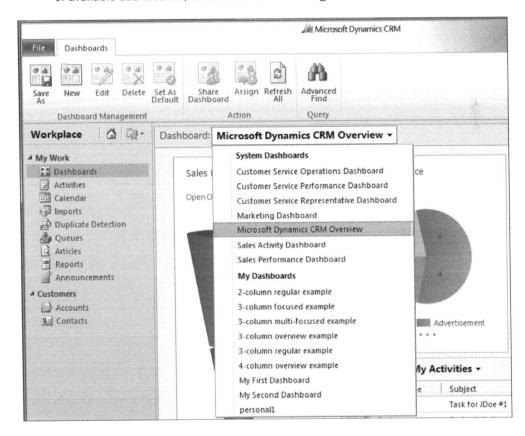

2. The user dashboards will be in the **My Dashboards** section of this list. Select one of the user dashboards that you created in the earlier chapters.

3. Once you have selected a user dashboard, the **Share Dashboard** button in the **Dashboards** toolbar will be enabled. Click on the **Share Dashboard** button, as shown in the following screenshot:

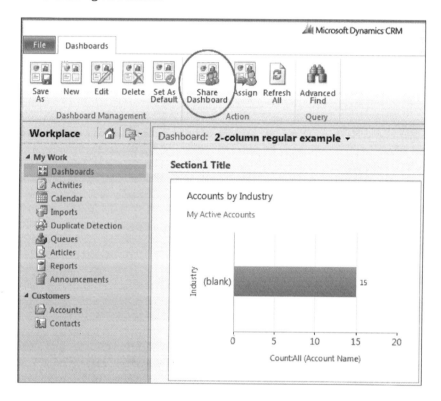

4. The Dynamics CRM sharing dialog will appear, the heading will read as **Who would you like to share the selected user dashboard with?**. Click on the **Add User/ Team** link to select individual users or entire teams. Share the current dashboard by selecting the **Read** privilege for each User or Team record, as shown in the following screenshot:

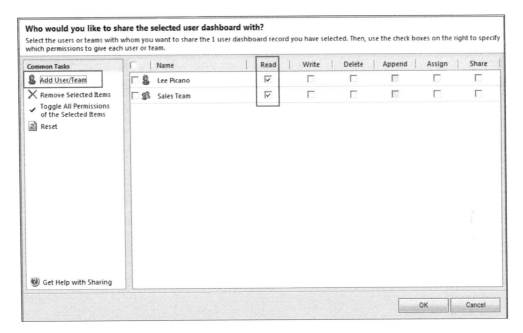

5. Once the **Read** privilege has been set, click on the **OK** button to apply the changes. The users or team members will now have access to this dashboard.

How it works...

The sharing of dashboards is only available for user dashboards in Dynamics CRM. The sharing rules (*who and how*) are stored with each individual dashboard. If you want to share multiple dashboards, you have to repeat the sharing steps for each dashboard.

There's more...

Sharing and assigning dashboards in Dynamics CRM comes with many different options for granting permissions to users and teams. This section provides details on the available permissions.

What about those other permissions?

When sharing a dashboard with other users in Dynamics CRM, there is a series of permissions that the owner can grant to other users and teams:

> ▸ The `Read` permission gives the user the ability to view the dashboard, although viewing the actual data in the dashboard is controlled through CRM Security Role assignments as mentioned in the following section. Similar to the rules around viewing reports, if the user does not have permissions to view `Accounts` in CRM (for example), then the dashboard will not show any data related to `Accounts`.

> ▸ The `Write` permission lets other users edit and modify the user dashboard. They could change the title and add or remove dashboard components with this permission.

> ▸ The `Delete` permission will allow other users to delete the dashboard from the system. This would remove it from the list of any user who has `Read` access to the dashboard. Deleting is covered in the *Deleting a user dashboard* recipe in *Chapter 5, Editing and Deleting Dashboards*.

> ▸ Having the `Assign` permission will allow users to assign ownership of this dashboard to themselves or other users in the CRM system. Assignment is covered in the *Assigning a user dashboard* recipe in this chapter.

> ▸ The `Share` permission lets users share access to this dashboard with other CRM users.

Security roles and dashboards in Dynamics CRM

When a dashboard is shared (for example, with a `Read` permission) with other users in Dynamics CRM, the dashboard will be accessible by the those users, but the data in the dashboard is still subject to the **access rights** defined by each user's assigned **security roles**.

As an example, there are two users in a system and `User1` creates a dashboard that contains `Opportunity` data. The dashboard is shared with `User2`, who does not have any `Read` access for `Opportunity` data in Dynamics CRM. Although `User2` can select the shared dashboard from the list of user dashboards, the data contents of the dashboard will be restricted from view (blank) because of their lack of permissions. `User2` would need to belong to a security role in Dynamics CRM that would grant them `Read` access rights for the `Opportunity` entity to get any value from the dashboard.

Assigning a user dashboard

After creating user dashboards for Dynamics CRM, the relevancy and even maintenance of the dashboard may become the responsibility of a different Dynamics CRM user. Instead of having to recreate the dashboard for the new user, Dynamics CRM supports **Assigning** ownership of user dashboards from one user to another.

Getting ready

This recipe assumes that there is more than just one user account in your Dynamics CRM system. Navigate to the **Dashboards** section in the Dynamics CRM 2011 **Workplace** area.

How to do it...

Carry out the following steps in order to complete this recipe:

1. Select the **Dashboards** link from the **Workplace** area.

2. The user dashboards will be in the **My Dashboards** section of this list. Select one of the user dashboards that you created in the earlier chapters, as shown in the following screenshot:

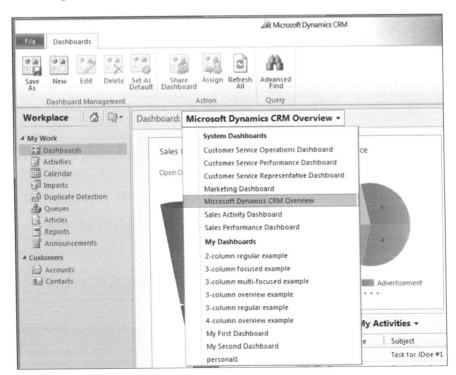

3. Once you have selected a user dashboard, the **Assign** button in the **Dashboards** toolbar will be enabled. Click on the **Assign** button, as shown in the following screenshot:

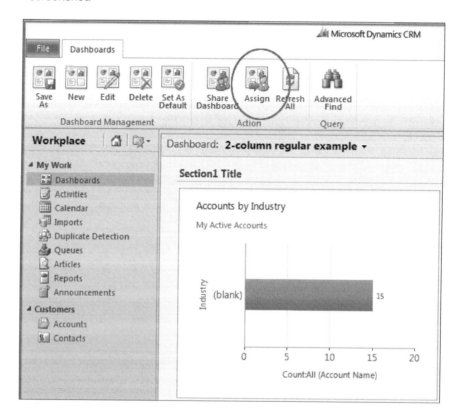

4. The assign dialog will appear with the heading **Assign User Dashboard**. Select the option labeled **Assign to another user or team**, and click on the lookup icon (*magnifying glass*) to select from a list of users and teams in the CRM system, as depicted in the following screenshot:

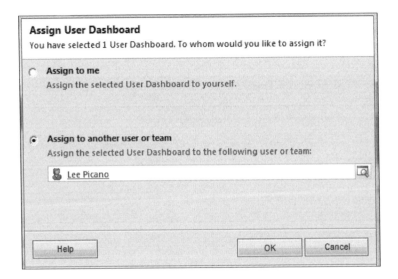

5. Once the user or team has been selected, click on the **OK** button to commit the changes. The dashboard now belongs to a different CRM user or team.

How it works...

User dashboards are *owned* by an individual Dynamics CRM user, not the CRM system as a whole. This means that the owner has the ability to decide who else can access the custom user dashboard. Any user that has been granted the `Assign` permission for the user dashboard can pass ownership of the Dashboard to a different user in the CRM system. Once the ownership of the dashboard is passed on to another user, the dashboard will be removed from the original owner's list of **My Dashboards**.

Copying an existing dashboard

When designing and building dashboards, you can use an existing dashboard as the starting template for a new dashboard. Using the **Save As** method, the user can copy an existing dashboard and rename it as something new.

Getting ready

Navigate to the **Dashboards** section in the Dynamics CRM 2011 **Workplace** area.

How to do it...

Carry out the following steps in order to complete this recipe:

1. Select the **Dashboards** link from the **Workplace** area.

2. Select the same personal dashboard we created in the earlier recipe (*Creating a user dashboard*) of *Chapter 3, Creating a Dashboard*.

3. From the **Dashboards** menu in the Dynamics CRM 2011 ribbon, click on the **Save As** button, as highlighted in the following screenshot:

4. A **Dashboard Properties** window will appear. Enter a different name for this copy of the new dashboard in the **Name** field, as shown in the following screenshot:

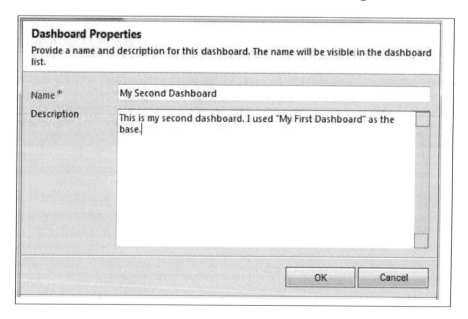

5. Once you click on the **OK** button, you will see your new dashboard displayed in the **Dashboard** list, as depicted in the following screenshot:

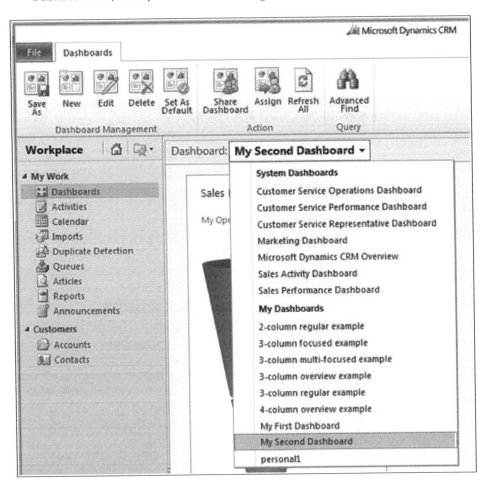

How it works...

The layout information for each component of the Dynamics CRM 2011 dashboard is stored as a record in the Dynamics CRM database. Using the **Save As** feature, Dynamics CRM creates a duplicate record of the database layout and identifies the new record with a unique name.

Using the **Save As** method to create a copy of the dashboard creates a clone of the original dashboard, but any changes made to the original dashboard will not be carried over into the cloned version of the dashboard.

5

Editing and Deleting Dashboards

In this chapter, we will cover:

- ▶ Editing a user dashboard
- ▶ Editing a system dashboard
- ▶ Deleting a user dashboard
- ▶ Deleting a system dashboard

Introduction

All of the chapters so far have focused on adding components to the dashboard. If you want to further refine the look of a dashboard, you will need to edit the components contained in the dashboard. This chapter shows how to edit user and system dashboards along with detailed information about the different properties that you can change on chart and list components.

Editing a user dashboard

After creating a user dashboard or getting access to another user dashboard (see *Chapter 4, Sharing and Assigning Dashboards*), you may still need to adjust the layout and settings of the dashboard.

Getting ready

Navigate to the **Dashboards** section in the Dynamics CRM 2011 **Workplace** area.

How to do it...

Carry out the following steps in order to complete this recipe:

1. Select the **Dashboards** link from the **Workplace** area.

2. Select one of your user dashboards (created in *Chapter 3, Creating a Dashboard*), as shown in the following screenshot:

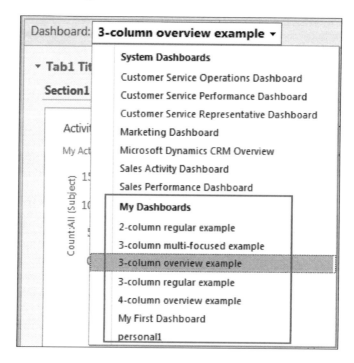

3. From the **Dashboards** menu in the Dynamics CRM 2011 ribbon, click on the **Edit** button, as highlighted in the following screenshot:

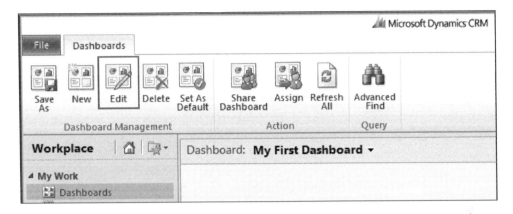

4. The dashboard editor screen will open, and the dashboard is now in **Edit** mode, as shown in the following screenshot:

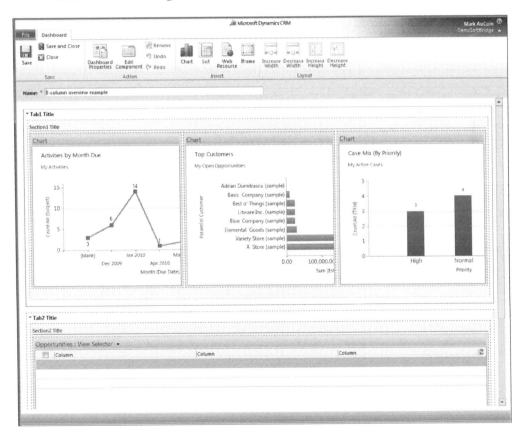

5. In order to edit the components on the dashboard, select a component by clicking on it with the mouse, and then click on the **Edit Component** ribbon button, as shown in the following screenshot:

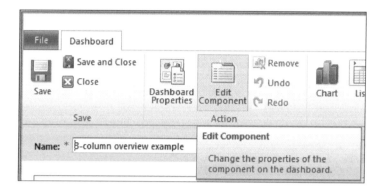

 Editing charts and lists has been covered in more detail in the recipes found in Chapter 3.

There's more...

Dynamics CRM has a robust security system that combines roles-based security and user permissions. These security settings allow the administrator to control access to data and functionality in the Dynamics CRM system.

Security roles for editing user dashboards

In order for a Dynamics CRM user to edit user dashboards, they must have a security role that grants the `Write` privilege for the **User Dashboard** entity. If a user's security role does not have this privilege, then they will not see the **Edit** button on the dashboard ribbon:

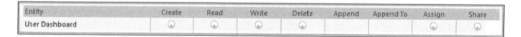

Editing a system dashboard

The system dashboards are intended to be viewed by all users of Dynamics CRM. These dashboards are created and managed by users with the **System Customizer** or **System Administrator** security roles (by default these roles have the `Write` privilege for the System Forms entity). Edits made to these dashboards are seen by all users.

Getting ready

Editing a System dashboard requires you to first navigate to the **Customization** section in the Dynamics CRM 2011 **Settings** area.

How to do it...

Carry out the following steps in order to complete this recipe:

1. From the **Customization** section, click on the **Customize the System** link, as shown in the following screenshot:

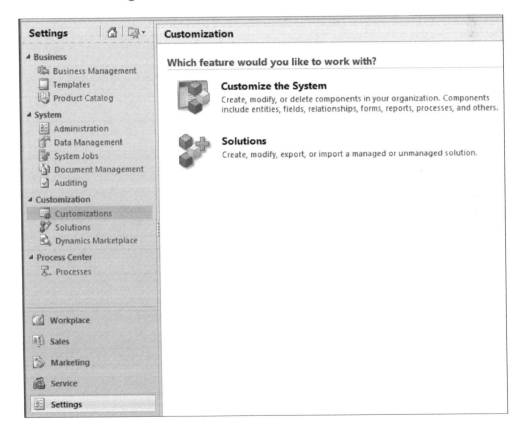

2. This will launch the solution editor dialog showing the **Default Solution** for Dynamics CRM 2011. Click on the **Dashboards** link located in the left-hand side navigation section, as shown in the following screenshot:

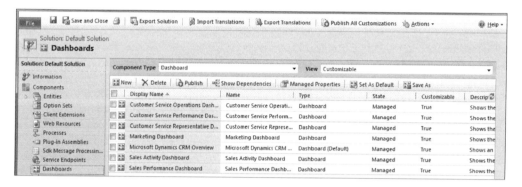

3. A listing of system dashboards will be shown. Double-click on the **Microsoft Dynamics CRM Overview** dashboard record. This will launch the dashboard editor screen.

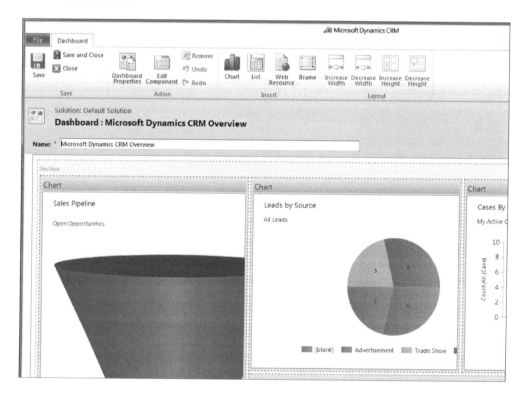

4. In order to edit the components on the dashboard, select a component by clicking on it with the mouse, and then click on the **Edit Component** ribbon button, as shown in the following screenshot:

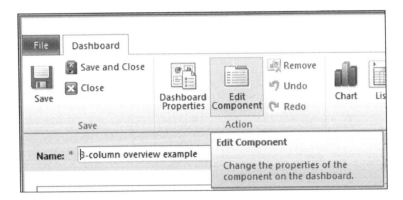

 Editing charts and lists has been covered in more detail in the recipes found in *Chapter 3, Creating a Dashboard.*

There's more...

Dynamics CRM has a robust security system that combines roles-based security and user permissions. These security settings allow the administrator to control access to data and functionality in the Dynamics CRM system.

Security roles for editing system dashboards

In order for a Dynamics CRM user to edit system dashboards, they must have a security role which grants the `Write` privilege for the **System Form** entity. If a user's security role does not have this privilege, then they will not be able to edit the dashboard when customizing the system. By default, the **System Forms** are only editable by users with the `System Customizer` or `System Administrator` security roles as they both have full privileges to the **System Form** entity.

Entity	Create	Read	Write	Delete	Append	Append To	Assign	Share
System Form	●	●	●	●				

Deleting a user dashboard

Creating new dashboards in Dynamics CRM is an excellent feature; however the on-going management of dashboards may require you to remove or **delete** some dashboards that are no longer needed. Deleting dashboards in Dynamics CRM cannot be undone; users should understand that deleting a dashboard is permanent.

Getting ready

Navigate to the **Dashboards** section in the Dynamics CRM 2011 **Workplace** area.

How to do it...

Carry out the following steps in order to complete this recipe:

1. Select the **Dashboards** link from the **Workplace** area, as shown in the following screenshot:

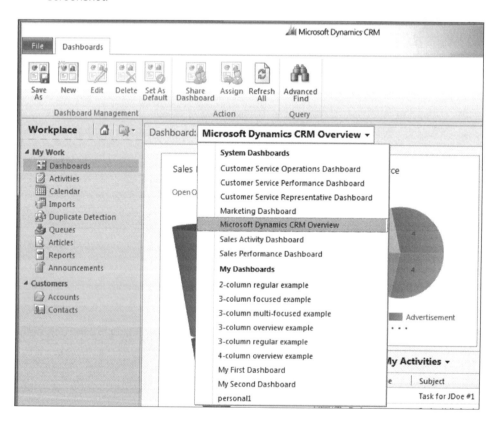

2. The user dashboards will be in the **My Dashboards** section of this list. Select one of the user dashboards that you created in the earlier chapters.

3. Once you have selected a user dashboard, the **Delete** button in the **Dashboards** toolbar will be enabled. Click on the **Delete** button, as shown in the following screenshot:

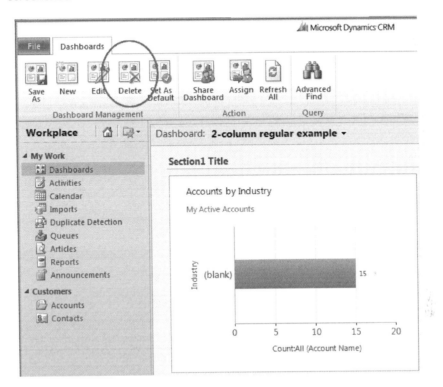

4. You will be prompted with a **Confirm Deletion** dialog. As the message in this dialog states, deleting a dashboard cannot be undone. If you want to continue and delete this dashboard from your system, click on the **OK** button. When the operation is finished, the screen will refresh and that dashboard will no longer be available.

Confirm Deletion
You have selected 1 Dashboard for deletion.

The system will delete this record. This action cannot be undone. To continue, click OK.

OK   Cancel

How it works...

The layouts and settings used to generate user dashboards are stored as records in the Dynamics CRM database. Deleting the dashboard will remove this record from the CRM database and cannot be reversed. Deleting the dashboard will only remove the dashboard layout and settings, not the associated data.

Deleting a system dashboard

Deleting a system dashboard will remove it from the list of available system dashboards for all of the Dynamics CRM users in a system. In order to delete a system dashboard, the user will need the **System Customizer** or **System Administrator** security roles.

Getting ready

Deleting a System dashboard requires you to navigate to the **Customization** section in the Dynamics CRM 2011 **Settings** area.

How to do it...

Carry out the following steps in order to complete this recipe:

1. From the **Customization** section, click on the **Customize the System** link, as shown in the following screenshot:

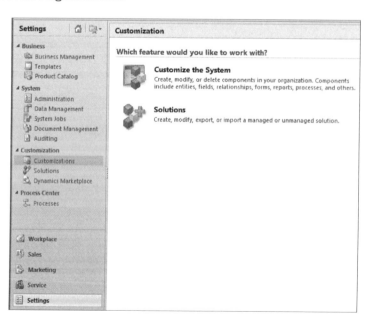

2. This will launch the solution editor dialog showing the **Default Solution** for Dynamics CRM 2011. Click on the **Dashboards** link located in the left-hand navigation section.

3. A listing of the current system dashboards will be shown. Select a system dashboard and click on the **Delete** button in the toolbar. I suggest you create a test system dashboard to play with, rather than deleting a system dashboard that might be of value.

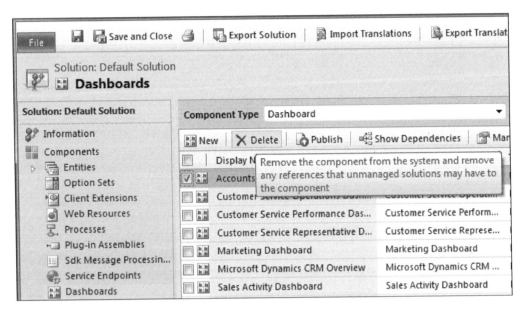

4. Dynamics CRM will prompt you for a confirmation. Clicking on **OK** under this dialog will delete and remove this system dashboard from your Dynamics CRM system. It cannot be undone, so be sure that you want to remove it first. Of course, none of the CRM data (`Contacts`, `Account`, and so on), Charts, Lists or Web Resources will be delete from the system. Only the dashboard, which refers to these components and data, will be removed.

Confirm Deletion
You have selected 1 Dashboard for deletion.

The system will delete this record. This action cannot be undone. To continue, click OK.

| OK | Cancel |

6
Adding IFrames and WebResources to Dashboards

In this chapter, we will cover:

- ▶ Adding an IFrame to a dashboard
- ▶ Editing an IFrame component
- ▶ Creating an HTML WebResource component
- ▶ Adding a WebResource to a dashboard
- ▶ Editing a WebResource component

Introduction

The dashboards in Dynamics CRM 2011 provide an excellent user experience with the use of charts and list components. In order to extend that experience the dashboards can also support the use of IFrames and WebResources. By definition, an IFrame component is an inline frame that allows you to display external objects and interact with them, such as static HTML or even interactive ASPX web components. A WebResource in Dynamics CRM refers to items such as Silverlight applications, XML files, JavaScript functions, and even self-contained HTML pages.

Adding an IFrame to a dashboard

This recipe will show you how to add an IFrame to a system dashboard. We will be adding an IFrame that links to a free **Microsoft FUSE Labs Social Gadget** that displays a tag cloud for the key phrase **Dynamics CRM**.

Getting ready

There is a difference in how user and system dashboards work with IFrames (explained in the *Restricting cross-frame scripting and User dashboards* section), so for this recipe, we will create a new system dashboard. Navigate to the **Customization** section in the Dynamics CRM 2011 **Settings** area.

How to do it...

Carry out the following steps in order to complete this recipe:

1. From the **Customization** section, click on the **Customize the System** link, as shown in the following screenshot:

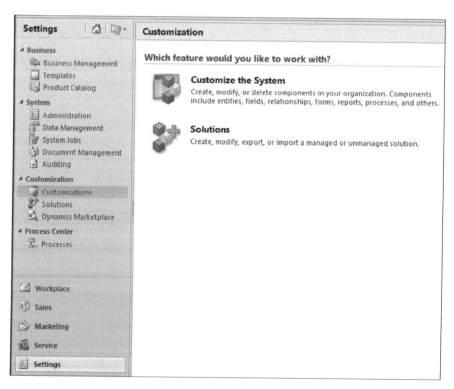

2. This will launch the **Solution Editor** dialog showing the **Default Solution** for Dynamics CRM 2011. Click on the **Dashboards** link located in the left-hand navigation section, as shown in the following screenshot:

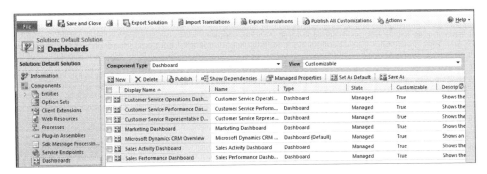

3. A listing of system dashboards will be shown. Click on the **New** button located in the list's toolbar. This will launch the **Select Dashboard Layout** screen.

4. Select a **2-Column Regular Dashboard** layout and click on the **Create** button. Provide a name, such as **iFrame and WebResource dashboard**. The IFrame and WebResource components will need lots of space, so I have adjusted the layout of my dashboard to only have one placeholder on each of the two rows. After you have adjusted the dashboard, click on the **Save** button, as shown in the following screenshot:

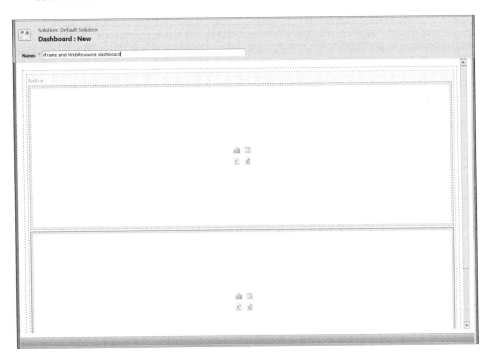

5. Click on the **Insert IFrame** icon located in the first component placeholder of the new dashboard. This will bring up the **Add an IFRAME** dialog:

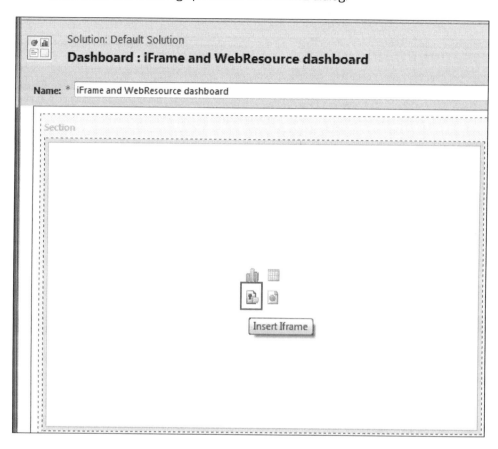

6. The **Name** field will already be filled in with a system-generated value, so we only have to provide a value for the **URL** field. Add the following value to the **URL** field:

```
http://embed.socialgadgets.fuselabs.com/Embed/
A?keyword=Dynamics CRM&ts=ThreeDays&ver=1.0
```

7. Next, make sure to uncheck the **Restrict cross-frame scripting** option located in the **Security** part of the dialog. A complete description of the option can be found later in this recipe. Click on the **OK** button to commit the changes:

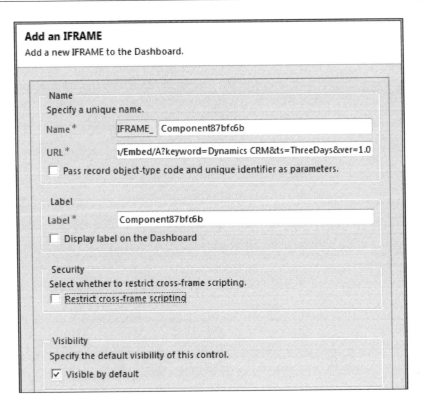

Add an IFRAME

Add a new IFRAME to the Dashboard.

Name

Specify a unique name.

Name *   IFRAME_   Component87bfc6b

URL *   /Embed/A?keyword=Dynamics CRM&ts=ThreeDays&ver=1.0

☐ Pass record object-type code and unique identifier as parameters.

Label

Label *   Component87bfc6b

☐ Display label on the Dashboard

Security

Select whether to restrict cross-frame scripting.

☐ Restrict cross-frame scripting

Visibility

Specify the default visibility of this control.

☑ Visible by default

8. Click on the **Save and Close** button on the dashboard editor ribbon bar. Select the new dashboard in the listing of system dashboards and click on the **Publish** button, as shown in the following screenshot:

9. In order to see the new dashboard with the IFrame component, navigate to the **Workplace** section of Dynamics CRM and select the new dashboard from the list of available dashboards:

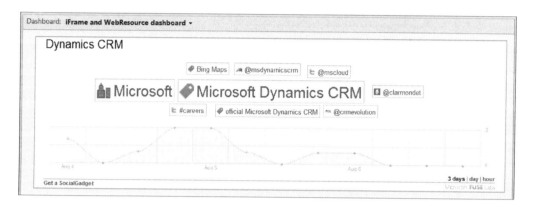

HTTP and HTTPS: Why do I get a secure content warning?

In order to meet security requirements, Dynamics CRM Online is served by an HTTPS channel (the same as online banking applications are) and when we mix that HTTPS content with an IFrame that contains HTTP content, as in this example, the users will get a security warning regarding the use of mixed content. Avoiding this message is outside the scope of this book, but there are supported ways to avoid getting this message when using Dynamics CRM Online. Please check with your systems administrator for directions, as this will involve modifying the client's Internet Explorer security settings to allow mixed content. This may go against your organization's security profiles, so it will need to be discussed before making these changes to the client machines.

The following screenshot shows a secure content warning, which you may get:

There's more...

Adding an IFrame component can be done very quickly using the dashboard designer. This section will discuss the other properties available for you when adding IFrame components.

Displaying a label for the IFrame

One of the options in the IFrame component lets you specify and display a label for the IFrame component. When this option is set, the text label will appear in the upper-left corner of the IFrame component. Note that making a label appear may result in the IFrame content being be misaligned, so it is better to test this before deployment. You can see in the following screenshot that the bottom of our **FuseLabs gadget** now gets chopped off when we show a label for the IFrame component:

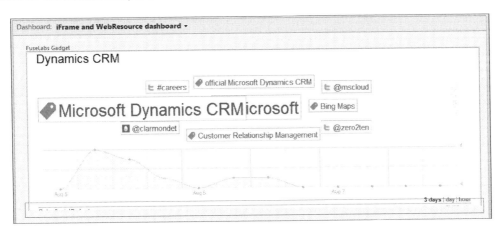

Passing object-type and GUID parameters

If the IFrame component is designed to reference dynamic content that can accept and process parameters from the Dynamics CRM system, then checking the **Pass record object-type code and unique identifier as parameters** option will pass the following information:

Parameter	Name	Description	Notes
typename	Entity Name	The name of the entity type hosting the IFrame.	Value is not passed from dashboard IFrame.
type	Entity Type Code	Integer value that represents the entity type. Assume they are unique for each CRM organization.	Value is not passed from dashboard IFrame.
id	GUID	The GUID value for a record.	Value is not passed from dashboard IFrame.
orgname	Organization Name	The unique name for the CRM organization.	Value is passed.
userlcid	User Language Code	The language code of the current user.	Value is passed.
orglcid	Organization Language Code	The base language code for the CRM organization.	Value is passed

Restricting cross-frame scripting and User dashboards

When building a User dashboard and adding an IFrame component, the **Restrict cross-frame scripting** checkbox field is disabled. Due to the security openings that happen when cross-frame scripting is enabled, User dashboards are not allowed to use this feature. Without using cross-frame scripting the IFrame can make references to content that exists on the same domain, but nothing outside the domain that may request information from the originator, such as reading the base URL.

The following link takes you to the Microsoft MSDN library to provide more information on cross-frame scripting and potential security concerns:

`http://msdn.microsoft.com/en-us/library/ms533028(v=VS.85).aspx`

The following screenshot shows a message that may appear when cross-frame scripting is being restricted:

This content cannot be displayed in a frame

To help protect the security of information you enter into this website, the publisher of this content does not allow it to be displayed in a frame.

Editing an IFrame component

Once you have created an IFrame component for a dashboard, editing the component is straightforward.

Getting ready

Navigate to the **Settings** area in Dynamics CRM 2011.

How to do it...

Carry out the following steps in order to complete this recipe:

1. Navigate to the **Customization** module in Dynamics CRM and click on the **Customize the System** link.

2. This will launch the **Solution Editor** dialog showing the **Default Solution** for Dynamics CRM 2011. Click on the **Dashboards** link located in the left-hand navigation section.

3. A listing of system dashboards will be shown. Double-click on the **IFrame and WebResource** dashboard record in this list. The dashboard editor screen will open:

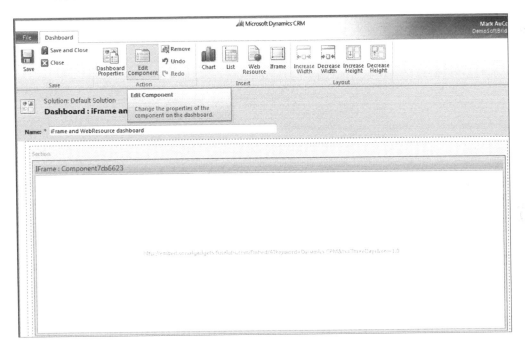

4. Select the **IFrame** component and click on the **Edit Component** button located in the ribbon toolbar. This will launch the **IFRAME Properties** dialog.

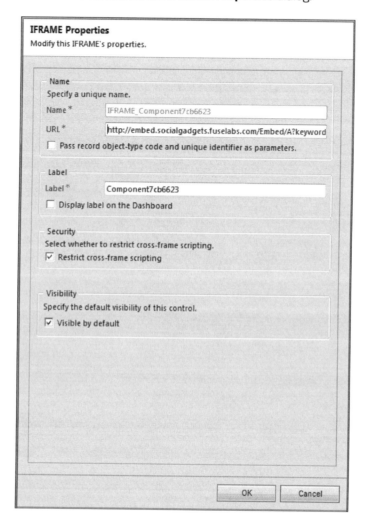

Creating an HTML WebResource component

Microsoft Dynamics CRM 2011 introduced the concept of WebResources. These components are files that are loaded and stored in the Dynamics CRM database as records. They each have a unique URL, and can be used together when creating a solution. Examples of WebResources include HTML files, JavaScript libraries, images, and Silverlight applications. ASPX files cannot be used as WebResources as no code can be processed and executed on the server directly. In this recipe, we will create an HTML WebResource that performs a simple area code and time zone lookup.

Getting ready

Navigate to the **Settings** area in Dynamics CRM 2011.

How to do it...

Carry out the following steps in order to complete this recipe:

1. Navigate to the **Customization** module in Dynamics CRM and click on the **Customize the System** link.

2. This will launch the **Solution Editor** dialog showing the **Default Solution** for Dynamics CRM 2011. Click on the **Web Resources** link located in the left-hand navigation list. Next, click on the **New** button in the toolbar, as shown in the following screenshot:

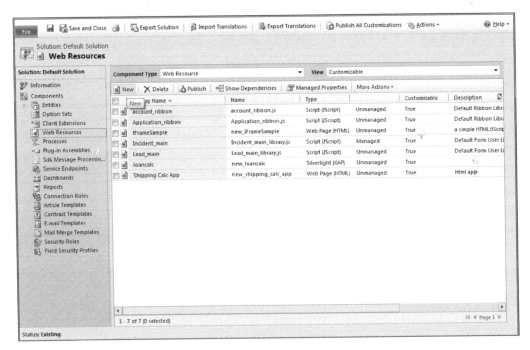

3. This will open the **Web Resource: New** dialog. Provide the following values for the fields on this form. Click the **Save** button on the ribbon toolbar to commit the changes.

Field	Value
Name	AreaCode_TimeZone_Search
Display Name	AreaCode TimeZone Search
Description	HTML application that Searches for AreaCode and returns related TimeZone information
Type	Web Page (HTML)
Language	English

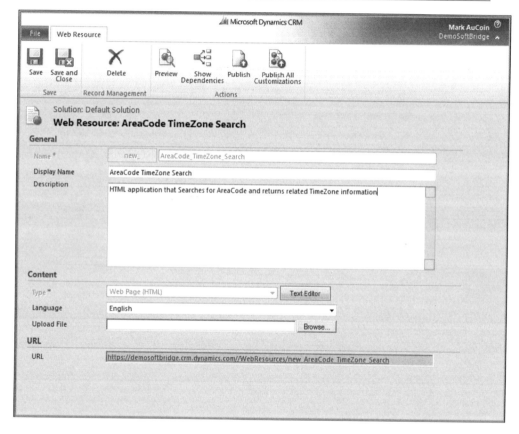

4. Click on the **Text Editor** button located next to the **Type** field. This will launch the **Edit Content** dialog. Switch the content to the **Source** view using the tabs along the top of the dialog:

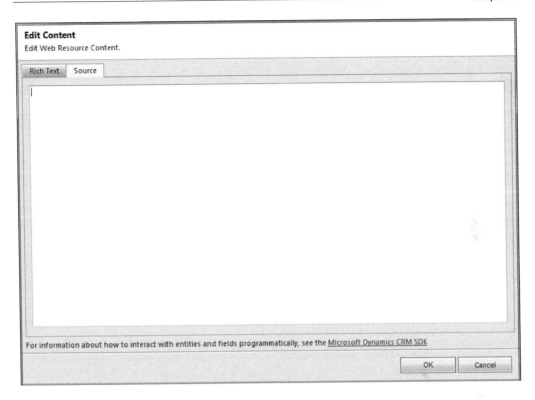

5. Erase whichever HTML content might be there by default, and then replace it with the following code snippet:

```
<!DOCTYPE html PUBLIC "-//W3C//DTD HTML 4.01//EN"
  "http://www.w3.org/TR/html4/strict.dtd">
<!-- <!DOCTYPE html PUBLIC "-//W3C//DTD HTML 4.01//EN"
  "http://www.w3.org/TR/html4/strict.dtd"> -->
<html>
  <head>
    <meta name="generator" content="HTML Tidy for Linux
      (vers 6 November 2007), see www.w3.org">
    <base>
    <meta>
    <title></title>

    <style type="text/css">
      div.c1 {COLOR: red}
    </style>
  </head>
  <body>
    <h2>Area Code and Timezone lookup</h2>
```

```html
<table>
  <tbody>
    <tr>
      <td>Enter Area Code:</td>
      <td><input name="txtAreaCode"></td>
      <td><input onclick="doSearch()" value="Search"
          type="button"></td>
    </tr>
  </tbody>
</table>
<div class="c1" id="divResult"></div>
<script type="text/javascript">
function doSearch()
{
  var areaCode = document.getElementById("txtAreaCode").value;
  if(areaCode == "416")
  {
    document.getElementById("divResult").
      innerHTML = "Toronto, Canada | EDT";
  }
  else
  {
    document.getElementById("divResult").
      innerHTML = "Area Code Not Found";
  }
}
</script>
</body>
</html>
```

6. Once you have entered the code, click the **OK** button to keep the new HTML. Click the **Preview** button on the ribbon toolbar to test out the HTML application, as shown in the following screenshot:

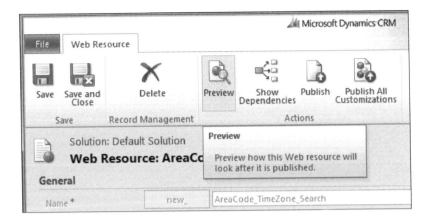

7. The HTML application will launch in a new window. To test out the script, enter **416** in the input box and then click the **Search** button. You should see **Toronto, Canada | EDT** as the result:

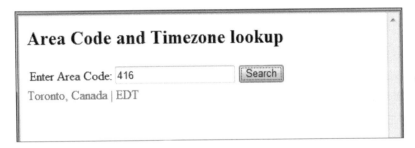

8. Once everything is tested and works properly, make sure to click the **Publish** button on the **WebResource Editor** dialog, so that this component will be available when we put it on a dashboard in the next recipe.

How it works...

The HTML code for this application is stored as a record in the Dynamics CRM database. It now has a unique relative URL that can be accessed by other WebResources and components in the system. For example, the HTML WebResource we just created can now be accessed from **SiteMaps** and other components in Dynamics CRM using the following relative URL:

```
/WebResources/new_AreaCode_TimeZone_Search
```

There's more...

Microsoft Dynamics CRM 2011 currently supports 10 types of WebResources for use in the system. However, only form-based WebResources can be used on a dashboard. A list of the various file types is given as follows:

File type	Supported (can be used on a dashboard)
Web Page (HTML)	Yes
Image (PNG)	Yes
Image (JPG)	Yes
Image (GIF)	Yes
Silverlight (XAP)	Yes
Image (ICO)	Yes
StyleSheet (XSL)	No
Style Sheet (CSS)	No
Script (JScript)	No
Data (XML)	No

Adding a WebResource to a dashboard

After creating a WebResource in the *Creating an HTML WebResource component* recipe, the following steps will add that WebResource to a dashboard.

Getting ready

Navigate to the **Settings** area in Dynamics CRM 2011.

How to do it...

Carry out the following steps in order to complete this recipe:

1. Navigate to the **Customization** module in Dynamics CRM and click on the **Customize the System** link.

2. This will launch the **Solution Editor** dialog showing the **Default Solution** for Dynamics CRM 2011. Click on the **Dashboards** link located in the left-hand navigation section.

3. A listing of system dashboards will be shown. Double-click on the **IFrame and WebResource dashboard** record in this list. The **Dashboard Editor** screen will open, as shown in the following screenshot:

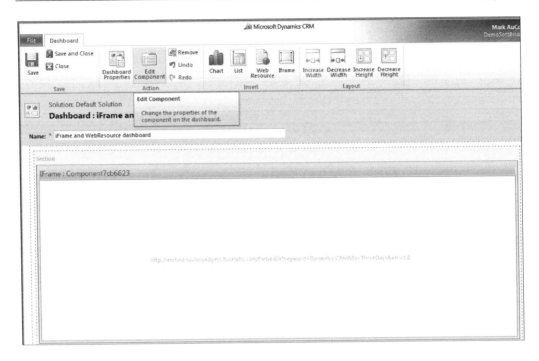

4. Select the empty placeholder component and click on the **Insert Web Resource** link as shown in the following screenshot:

5. This will launch the **Add Web Resource** dialog. Click on the lookup icon to see a listing of the available form-enabled WebResources for this dashboard:

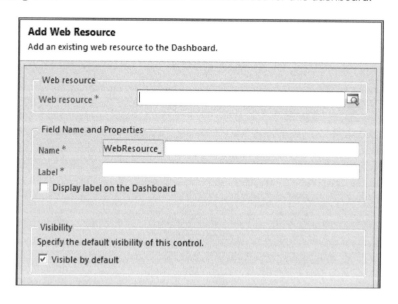

6. Locate and select the **new_AreaCode_TimeZone_Search** WebResource from the list and then click the **OK** button, as shown in the following screenshot:

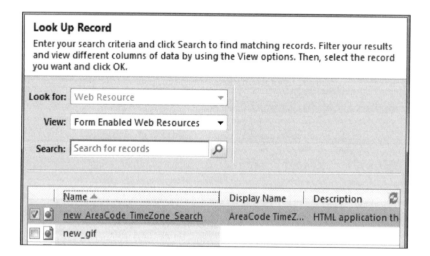

7. Once the WebResource has been selected, provide a value for the **Name** and **Label** fields. Click on the **OK** button to save the settings:

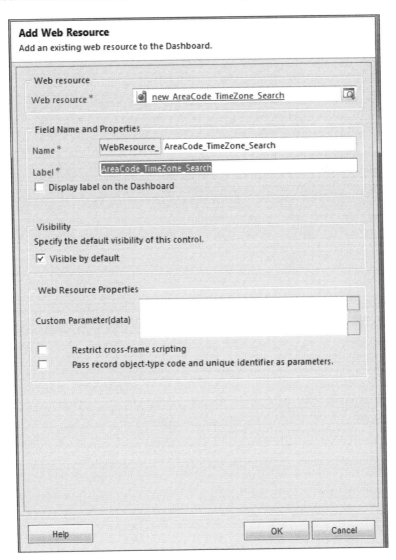

8. Now the dashboard will have two components on it, the first is an IFrame and the second is the new WebResource. Click on the **Save and Close** button on the ribbon toolbar:

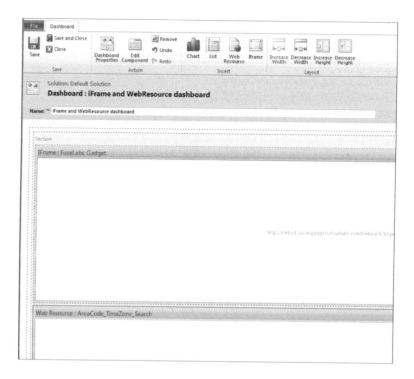

9. Once you have published all the changes, navigate to the **Dashboards** section in the **Workplace** area and view the updated dashboard, shown in the following screenshot:

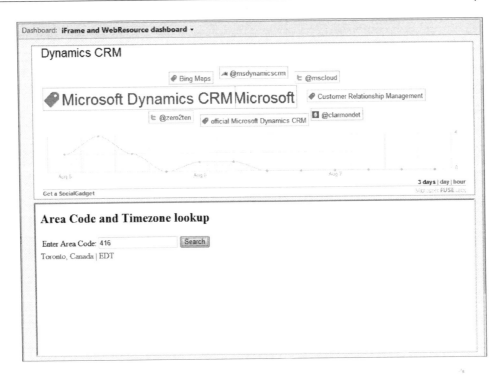

There's more...

Adding a WebResource to Dynamics CRM allows you to extend the feature set and functionality of your CRM solution. WebResources can also be designed to interact with your system by accepting parameters at runtime.

Passing a custom parameter (data) to a WebResource

The Dynamics CRM platform can also pass parameters to the HTML and Silverlight WebResources using the **data** parameter to retrieve information. This is the only custom parameter that is recognized by the WebResources and it is set in the **Web Resource Properties** window, shown in the following screenshot. If you need to send multiple values through this single parameter, you will need to encode them and have the target WebResource split and decode them at runtime:

Editing a WebResource component

Once you have placed a WebResource component on the dashboard, editing the component is straightforward.

Getting ready

Navigate to the **Settings** area in Dynamics CRM 2011.

How to do it...

Carry out the following steps in order to complete this recipe:

1. Navigate to the **Customization** module in Dynamics CRM and click on the **Customize the System** link.

2. This will launch the **Solution Editor** dialog showing the **Default Solution** for Dynamics CRM 2011. Click on the **Dashboards** link located in the left-hand navigation section.

3. A listing of system dashboards will be shown. Double-click on the **IFrame and WebResource** dashboard record in this list. The **Dashboard Editor** screen will open, as shown in the following screenshot:

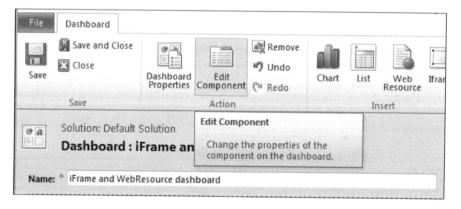

4. Select the WebResource component and click the **Edit Component** button located in the ribbon toolbar; this will launch the **Web Resource Properties** dialog:

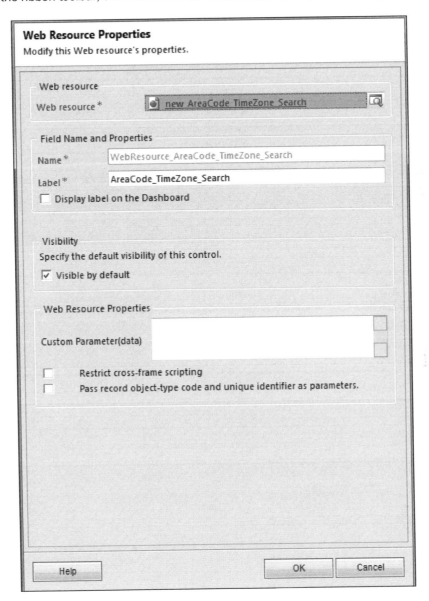

7
Advanced Dashboards

In this chapter, we will cover:

- ▸ Exporting a dashboard from Dynamics CRM
- ▸ Creating a new dashboard layout using FormXML
- ▸ Importing a dashboard into Dynamics CRM
- ▸ Building a CRM Organization Overview dashboard
- ▸ Installing the free Dashboard Reports control
- ▸ Showing reports on a Dynamics CRM dashboard

Introduction

Creating and editing dashboards using the Dynamics CRM interface definitely gives developers and administrators many options for configuring great dashboards. However some customizations may require you to edit or create a dashboard outside of the Dynamics CRM interface to get results not available through the interface. This chapter explains how to work directly with the **FormXML** element to produce unique dashboards.

Exporting a dashboard from Dynamics CRM

In order to work with a dashboard's Form XML using Microsoft Visual Studio, first you have to export the existing Dashboard using a Solution Package in Dynamics CRM. This recipe will cover exporting the Dashboard and then accessing the Form XML. An in-depth review of importing and exporting Solution Packages is outside the scope of this book, but this section covers the necessary steps to complete the recipe.

Getting ready

This recipe will be exporting the standard **Dynamics CRM Overview** dashboard that comes pre-installed with Dynamics CRM 2011. Navigate to the **Solutions** section in the Dynamics CRM 2011 **Settings** area.

How to do it...

Carry out the following steps in order to complete this recipe:

1. Once you have navigated to the **Solutions** section in the **Settings** area, click on the **New** button to create a blank solution for this recipe, as shown in the following screenshot:

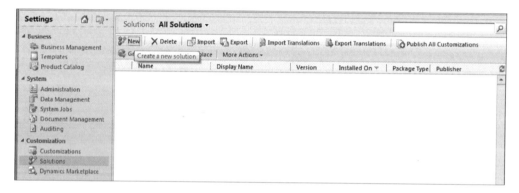

2. A screen will open for the new solution, as shown in the following screenshot. Fill in the required fields as listed in the following table and then click the **Save** button to commit the changes.

Field	Value	Notes
Display Name	**Dynamics CRM Overview Dashboard**	
Name	**DynamicsCRMOverviewDashboard**	This value will be generated from the Display Name field value will be generated
Publisher	**Default Publisher for orgebeb7**	There will be at least one default publisher for your CRM instance value will be generated
Version	**1.0**	

3. Once you have saved the solution package, click on the **Dashboards** area located in the left-hand navigation of the screen. Next, click on the **Add Existing** button, as shown in the following screenshot:

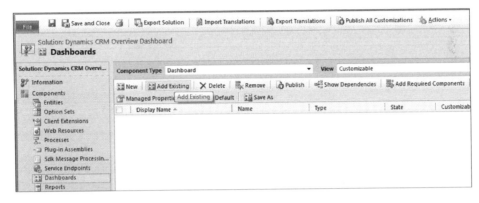

4. A **Select solution components** screen will appear that shows a list of all the dashboards currently published in the application. Locate and select the **Microsoft Dynamics CRM Overview** dashboard and then click on the **OK** button:

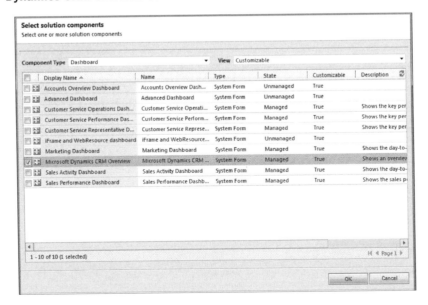

5. As the selected dashboard displays data for the different entities (record types) in Dynamics CRM, the **Missing Required Components** dialog will appear and prompt you to include the component types displayed on the dashboard in your solution package. However, if you are exporting a completely blank dashboard, then you will not be prompted to include missing required components. In this case, since we are extracting the dashboard to modify it and then load back into the same solution, you can skip this prompt by selecting the **No, do not include required components** option and then click on the **OK** button. Please note, if you were following proper development guidelines then you would include all missing required components in the solution as well:

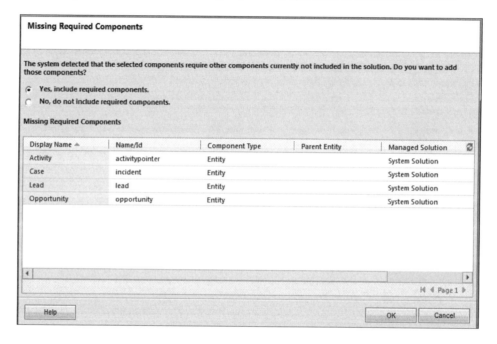

6. Now that your solution package contains the **Microsoft Dynamics CRM Overview** dashboard, you can export the solution by clicking on the **Export Solution** button located on the window toolbar, as shown in the following screenshot:

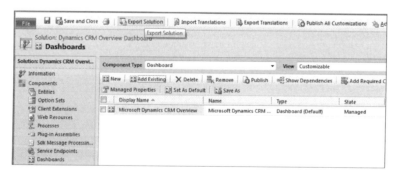

7. The first step in the Export Solution process is navigating to the **Publish Customizations** screen. This screen gives you a chance to publish any and all customizations that you may have worked on in the solution by clicking on the **Publish All Customizations** button. Since we have not made any changes yet, you can skip this step by clicking on the **Next** button. Please note that in order to follow best practices in a real development process, you should click on the **Publish All Customizations** button to ensure that you are getting the latest version of all components:

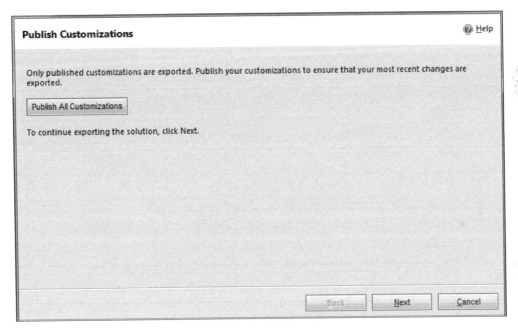

8. If the dashboard contains any chart or list components, the **Missing Required Components** screen will prompt you to include any of the components needed for this solution package.

As mentioned earlier, this step is a warning to remind you that if you try to import a solution package and the required components are missing then the import process will fail. Since, we are editing an existing dashboard and re-importing it right away, you can skip this screen by clicking on the **Next** button:

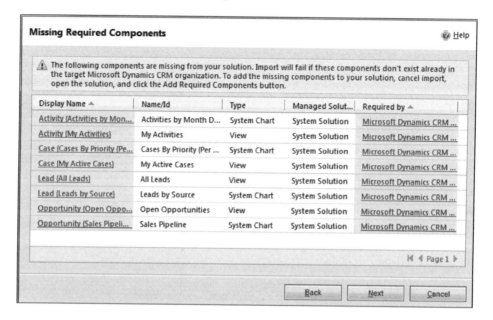

9. The next screen will be the **Export System Settings (Advanced)** dialog. You will not need to include any of these settings in the solution package. Click on the **Next** button to continue further:

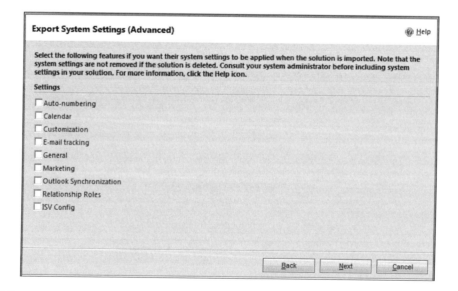

10. The final screen is the **Package Type** dialog, which asks you to select between an **Unmanaged** or **Managed** solution export. Delving into the differences between unmanaged and managed solutions in Dynamics CRM is outside the scope of this book, so for this recipe select the **Unmanaged** option and then click on the **Export** button, as shown in the following screenshot:

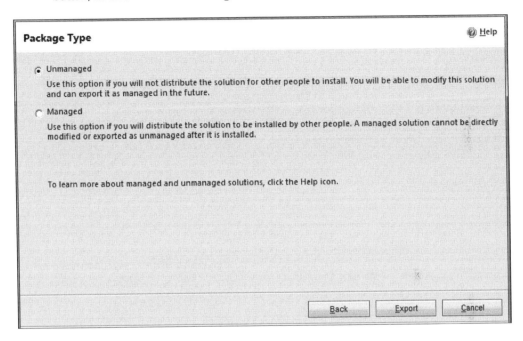

11. After you click on the **Export** button, the dialog will disappear. Dynamics CRM is combining all the components required to export and creating a ZIP file for download. This process may take a few seconds to complete.

12. Save the ZIP file to a location on your computer. Locate the file using Windows Explorer and unzip the contents. The contents of the solution package are three XML files.

Filename	Description	Notes
solution.xml	Contains the details of the solution package including publisher information and a listing of any missing or key dependencies.	Do not edit this file.
[Content_Types].xml	Standard Microsoft export file that identifies the content of the solution. Since this is all XML there will be only one content type listed.	Do not edit this file.
customizations.xml	This file contains all of the content and mark-up that will need to be changed.	Edit this file.

13. Open the `customizations.xml` file in an XML editor, as shown in the following screenshot, so that you can browse the XML content to get familiar with how a dashboard is constructed using `FormXML`. Since this recipe started by using a dashboard that already had components on it, the Form XML will contain a lot of information. If you started with a new, empty dashboard, then the `FormXML` would be less complex:

 We are using Visual Studio to do XML editing in these examples.

```xml
customizations.xml
 1  <ImportExportXml xmlns:xsi="http://www.w3.org/2001/XMLSchema-instance">
 2    <Entities></Entities>
 3    <Roles></Roles>
 4    <Workflows></Workflows>
 5    <FieldSecurityProfiles></FieldSecurityProfiles>
 6    <Templates />
 7    <EntityMaps />
 8    <EntityRelationships />
 9    <OrganizationSettings />
10    <optionsets />
11    <Dashboards>
12      <Dashboard>
13        <LocalizedNames>
14          <LocalizedName description="Microsoft Dynamics CRM Overview" languagecode="1033" />
15        </LocalizedNames>
16        <Descriptions>
17          <Description description="Shows an overview of your data in Microsoft Dynamics CRM.
18        </Descriptions>
19        <FormId>{ee50a18b-3f88-df11-8d93-00155db1891a}</FormId>
20        <IsDefault>1</IsDefault>
21        <FormXml>
22          <forms type="dashboard">
```

Backup, Backup, Backup!

Once you have downloaded the compressed `Solution Package` file, a best practice is to create a backup of that file by adding a descriptive label such as `[filename]_base_[date].zip` and either load it on your organization's source code repository or at least create a backup folder on your machine. This will save you from trying to reverse customizations if you make any major mistakes.

Creating a new dashboard layout using FormXML

In *Chapter 3, Creating a Dashboard*, readers were introduced to the six different dashboard layouts that are provided using the Dynamics CRM dashboard editor. This recipe will show the reader how to quickly create a custom layout that includes three tab sections.

Getting ready

This recipe will create a new dashboard and export a solution package. Please refer to the previous recipe *Exporting a dashboard from Dynamics CRM* for detailed information on how to export the solution package.

How to do it...

Carry out the following steps in order to complete this recipe:

1. Navigate to the **Solutions** section in the **Settings** area. Create a new solution package with the following values and then save the solution package.

Field	Value	Notes
Display Name	**CRM Organization Overview Dashboard**	
Name	**CRMOrganizationOverviewDashboard**	This value will be generated from the Display Name field.
Publisher	**Default Publisher for orgebeb7**	There will be at least 1 default publisher for your CRM instance.
Version	**1.0**	

2. After saving the changes, navigate to the solution package's **Dashboard** area and create a new dashboard by clicking on the **New** button in the toolbar, as shown in the following screenshot:

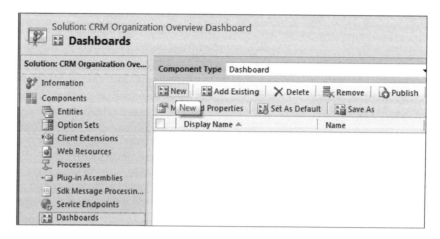

3. Create a new dashboard using the **3-Column Overview Dashboard** layout. If needed then refer to *Chapter 3, Creating a Dashboard*, as it covers the steps needed to create a dashboard:

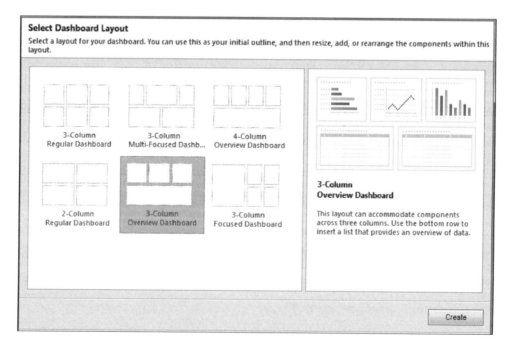

4. Do not add any components to the dashboard. Fill in the **Name** field with **CRM Organization Overview Dashboard**. Click on the **Save and Close** button to commit the changes and close the **Dashboard Editor** screen:

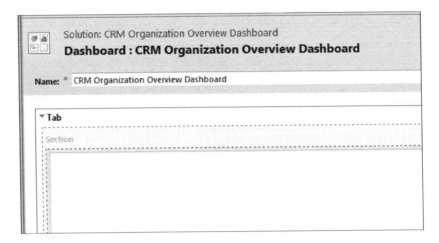

5. From the **Solution Package** screen, click on the **Export Solution** button, as shown in the following screenshot, and save the ZIP file to your machine. If needed, refer to the previous recipe, *Exporting a Dashboard from Dynamics CRM*, which covers all the steps involved in exporting a solution:

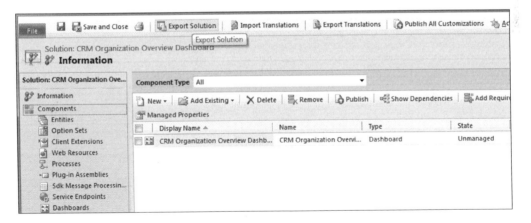

6. Once the file has downloaded, extract the contents of the ZIP file, and then open the `customizations.xml` file in an XML editor such as Visual Studio. Only the `<Dashboards>` element has data; this is where the changes will be made:

```
customizations.xml*
  1 <ImportExportXml xmlns:xsi="http://www.w3.org/2001/XMLSchema-instance">
  2     <Entities></Entities>
  3     <Roles></Roles>
  4     <Workflows></Workflows>
  5     <FieldSecurityProfiles></FieldSecurityProfiles>
  6     <Templates />
  7     <EntityMaps />
  8     <EntityRelationships />
  9     <OrganizationSettings />
 10     <optionsets />
 11     <Dashboards>
 12         <Dashboard>
 13             <LocalizedNames>
 14                 <LocalizedName description="CRM Organization Overview Dashboard" languagecode="1033" />
 15             </LocalizedNames>
 16             <FormId>{3ae49ee2-edd1-e011-83d3-1cc1def13751}</FormId>
 17             <IsCustomizable>1</IsCustomizable>
 18             <IsDefault>0</IsDefault>
 19             <FormXml>...</FormXml>
145         </Dashboard>
146     </Dashboards>
147     <Languages>...</Languages>
150 </ImportExportXml>
```

7. To create a dashboard with a total of three tabs that will be used for **Sales**, **Service**, and **Activity data**, we need to modify the `FormXML` elements directly. Locate and copy the last `<tab>` element in the `<tabs>` collection. Refer to the *Understanding FormXML* section later in this recipe for more information about the schema used in `FormXML` dashboards:

8. Paste the copied `<tab>` element, so that there are a total of three `<tab>` elements in the `<tabs>` collection, as shown in the following screenshot:

```
<ImportExportXml xmlns:xsi="http://www.w3.org/2001/XMLSchema-instance">
    <Entities></Entities>
    <Roles></Roles>
    <Workflows></Workflows>
    <FieldSecurityProfiles></FieldSecurityProfiles>
    <Templates />
    <EntityMaps />
    <EntityRelationships />
    <OrganizationSettings />
    <optionsets />
    <Dashboards>
        <Dashboard>
            <LocalizedNames>
                <LocalizedName description="CRM Organization Overview Dashboard" languagecode="1033" />
            </LocalizedNames>
            <FormId>{3ae49ee2-edd1-e011-83d3-1cc1def13751}</FormId>
            <IsCustomizable>1</IsCustomizable>
            <IsDefault>0</IsDefault>
            <FormXml>
                <forms type="dashboard">
                    <form>
                        <tabs>
                            <tab showlabel="true" verticallayout="true" id="{02d8ed07-4e8a-">...</tab>
                            <tab showlabel="true" verticallayout="true" id="{6949d91e-67a1-">...</tab>
                            <tab showlabel="true" verticallayout="true" id="{39083292-84f9-">...</tab>
                        </tabs>
                    </form>
                </forms>
            </FormXml>
        </Dashboard>
    </Dashboards>
    <Languages>...</Languages>
</ImportExportXml>
```

9. Expand the new **<tab>** element in your XML editor, so that you can modify the attributes directly. You will need to generate three new **GUID** values for the `<tab>` element's `id` attributes. If you are using Microsoft Visual Studio, there is a **Create GUID** function located under the **Tools** menu:

```
<tab showlabel="true" verticallayout="true" id="{6949d91e-67a1-4bc3-9f52-82c0eb331060}">
    <labels>
        <label description="Tab" languagecode="1033" />
    </labels>
    <columns>
        <column width="100%">
            <sections>
                <section showlabel="false" showbar="false" columns="111" id="{2a8664e1-1889-47a5-8351-f2072ed49f6c}">
                    <labels>
                        <label description="Section" languagecode="1033" />
                    </labels>
                    <rows>
                        <row>
                            <cell colspan="3" rowspan="12" showlabel="false" ispreviewcell="true" id="{a30c8e11-beb0-47bc-9d83-9aed5f9e2f43}">
                                <labels>
                                    <label description="" languagecode="1033" />
                                </labels>
                            </cell>
                        </row>
                        <row></row>
                        <row></row>
                        <row></row>
                        <row></row>
                        <row></row>
                        <row></row>
                        <row></row>
                        <row></row>
                        <row></row>
                        <row></row>
                    </rows>
                </section>
            </sections>
        </column>
    </columns>
</tab>
```

❑ The first GUID replaces the `id` attribute value for the `<tab>` element:

```
<tab showlabel="true" verticallayout="true" id="{39083292-84f9-4ccd-90cf-2a38c51654bf}">
```

❑ The second GUID replaces the `id` attribute value for the `<section>` element:

```
<section showlabel="false" showbar="false" columns="111" id="{85e7ab08-9d5a-4d35-b1dc-376509866588}">
```

❑ The third GUID replaces the `id` attribute value for the `<cell>` element:

```
<cell colspan="3" rowspan="12" showlabel="false" ispreviewcell="true" id="{affb9e14-8502-42ce-a983-5e92755a4970}">
```

10. The dashboard customizations are complete for the scope of this recipe. A new solution package `.zip` will need to be created, so that it can be imported back into Dynamics CRM. Using Windows Explorer, locate the three files that were unzipped in the earlier steps and compress them into a new `.zip` file.

Filename Versioning

It is a good suggestion to version compressed files to keep track of the newest one when importing. For example, the original export package was named `CRMOrganizationOverviewDashboard_1_0.zip` and after the changes were made, the new compressed file for import was named `CRMOrganizationOverviewDashboard_1_1.zip`.

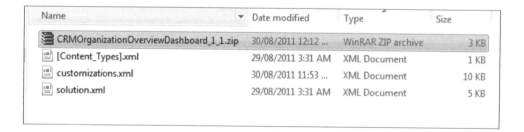

Name	Date modified	Type	Size
CRMOrganizationOverviewDashboard_1_1.zip	30/08/2011 12:12 ...	WinRAR ZIP archive	3 KB
[Content_Types].xml	29/08/2011 3:31 AM	XML Document	1 KB
customizations.xml	30/08/2011 11:53 ...	XML Document	10 KB
solution.xml	29/08/2011 3:31 AM	XML Document	5 KB

Refer to the next recipe *Importing a dashboard into Dynamics CRM* for instructions on how to import a modified solution package.

Although there are more `FormXML` changes that can be made using the XML editor such as changing cell heights and widths, or modifying text labels, the goal of this recipe was to create a dashboard layout that wasn't possible through the Dynamics CRM Dashboard Editor interface. The Dynamics CRM dashboard editor is still the preferred tool for adding charts, lists, and other components, as it provides a fast and easy **WYSIWYG** editor.

Using the FormXML.xsd schema file to validate customizations

Microsoft Dynamics CRM comes with a freely downloadable feature-rich SDK that provides detailed in-depth information about the inner working of Dynamics CRM along with useful code samples and templates to speed up the learning process. You can locate the latest version of the SDK on Microsoft's website or by searching for Dynamics CRM SDK in your favorite search engine.

If you have downloaded the **Microsoft Dynamics CRM 2011 SDK** there will be series of XSD schema files available for use. The files are located in the `SDK\Schemas` folder. Including the XSD files in your XML editor as a validation schema allows you to validate and correct any changes that you make to the XML before importing back into the solution again.

In order to use the Dynamics CRM schema files, include a reference to the `customizationssolution.xml` file. This is the top-level file for the `customizations.xml` and will pull in the Dashboard `FormXML` information as well. Depending on the XML editor you are using, the instructions for including an XML reference file may vary. Please refer to your product documentation for more information.

Understanding FormXML

The following section provides a simple outline of `FormXML`, as it is used in dashboards in Dynamics CRM. In order to get an in-depth review of the many different elements and attributes available in the Form XML mark-up, you should download the Microsoft Dynamics CRM SDK or search the online MSDN libraries for more information.

```
<Dashboards>
  <Dashboard>
    <FormId>{GUID}</FormId>
    <FormXml>
      <forms>
        <form>
          <tabs>
            <tab id="{GUID}">
              <label/>
              <columns>
                <column>
                  <sections>
```

```
<section id="{GUID}">
  <label/>
  <rows>
    <row>
      <cell id="{GUID}">
        <label/>
        <control classid="{GUID}">
          <parameters>
            <VisualizationId/>
            <ViewId/>
            ...etc...
          </parameters>
        </control>
      </cell>
    </row>
  </rows>
</section>
</sections>
</column>
</columns>
</tab>
</tabs>
</form>
</forms>
</FormXml>
</Dashboard>
</Dashboards>
```

Importing a dashboard into Dynamics CRM

This recipe includes the steps required to import and publish a **solution package** that contains the edited dashboard layout from the previous recipe.

Getting ready

Once you have exported and edited the dashboard as outlined in the other recipes in this chapter, navigate to the **Solutions** section in the Dynamics CRM 2011 **Settings** area.

How to do it...

Carry out the following steps in order to complete this recipe:

1. Once you have navigated to the **Solutions** section in the **Settings** area, click on the **Import** button in the toolbar, as shown in the following screenshot:

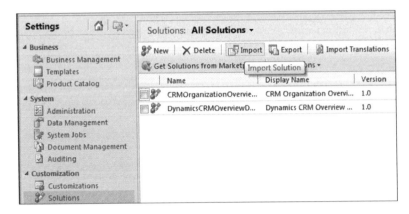

2. The **Select Solution Package** screen will appear and prompt you to locate the new compressed solution package file (`.zip` or `.cab` format) that you created earlier in the *Creating a new Dashboard layout using FormXML* recipe. Click on the **Browse** button to find your solution package and select it for import:

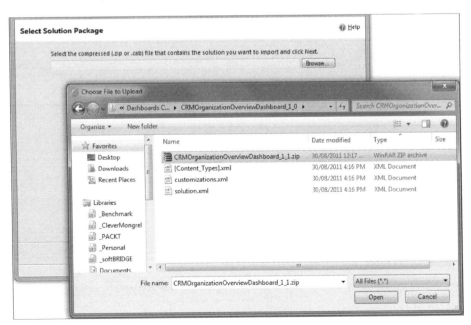

3. After you have selected the `.zip` file and clicked on the **Next** button, the **Solution Information** screen will appear. This page reminds you that unmanaged solution packages cannot be uninstalled. If you want to inspect the contents of the solution package, click on the **View solution package details** button to see that information. Click on the **Next** button to continue:

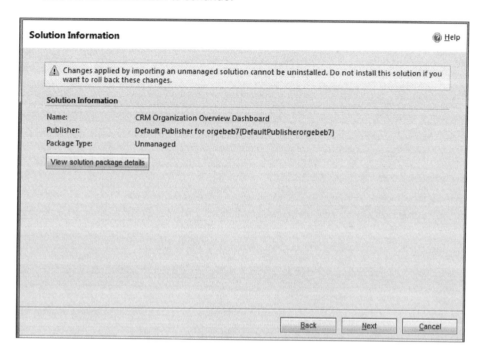

4. A small import progress screen will appear, shown in the following screenshot. This checks the contents of the import ZIP to make sure everything is in the proper order and all required files have been included:

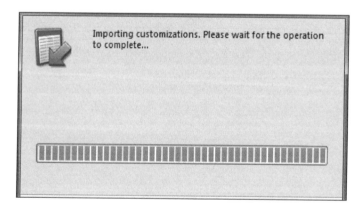

5. Once the import is finished, you will see the **Importing Solution** screen. If there errors in the solution package they will be displayed in this screen, and you can click the **Download Log File** button to see those messages. Click the **Close** button to dismiss this dialog.

Publish All Customizations

If you click on the **Publish All Customizations** button, it will publish the new dashboard and make it available for all your system users. This will not cause any harm, but since we still have to update the contents of the dashboard there is no reason to do this yet as users would see an incomplete dashboard.

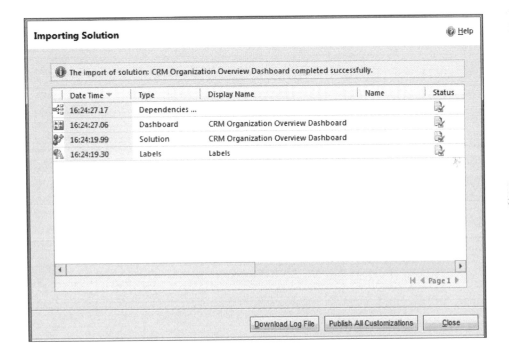

6. Now the updated dashboard layout has been loaded into Dynamics CRM. In order to see the new layout, open the CRM Organization Overview Dashboard solution package, navigate to the **Dashboards** list and open the dashboard (double-click) to see it in the **Dynamics CRM Dashboard Editor** screen. The dashboard should have three tab regions, which would not be possible using the standard CRM Dashboard Editor:

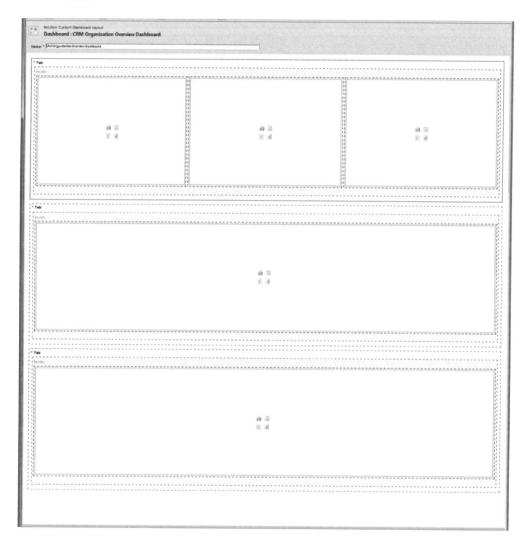

Building a CRM Organization Overview dashboard

Throughout this chapter, we have been working towards creating a new dashboard layout that supports three tab areas with a total of six dashboard components. In this recipe, we will configure an organization overview dashboard that shows three tabs of information.

Getting ready

Use the **CRM Organization Overview Dashboard** solution package created earlier in this chapter by navigating to the **Dashboards** list.

How to do it...

Carry out the following steps in order to complete this recipe:

1. Open the **CRM Organization Overview Dashboard** from the solution package. This will launch the **Dynamics CRM Dashboard Editor** screen. The dashboard will have three main tabs with one section in each tab.

2. Select the first tab and click on the **Edit Component** button located in the toolbar, as shown in the following screenshot:

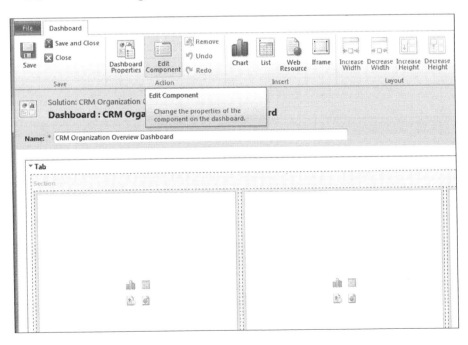

3. The **Tab Properties** dialog will appear. Change the **Label** field value to **Sales** and then click on the **OK** button:

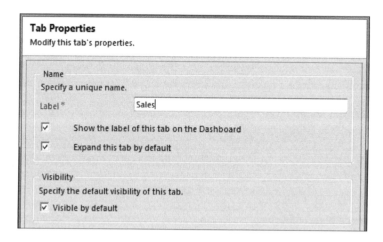

4. In the **Sales** tab, select the third component placeholder and click on the **Remove** button in the toolbar, as shown in the following screenshot:

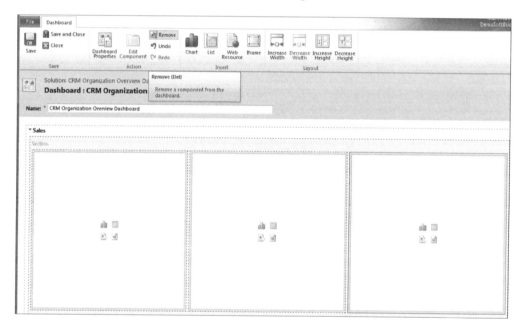

5. In the **Sales** tab, select the first component placeholder and add a new chart. Select the **Sales Pipeline** chart using the **My Open Opportunities** view for the **Opportunity** entity. Now, click on the **OK** button:

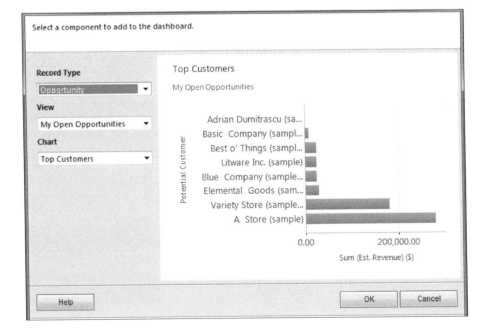

6. Select the second component placeholder and add a new chart. Select the **Top Customers** chart using the **My Open Opportunities** view for the **Opportunity** entity and click on the **OK** button, as shown in the following screenshot:

7. Selecting the second chart, click on the **Increase Width** button located in the toolbar. This will make the new chart take up two cell spaces and fill in the section, as shown in the following screenshot:

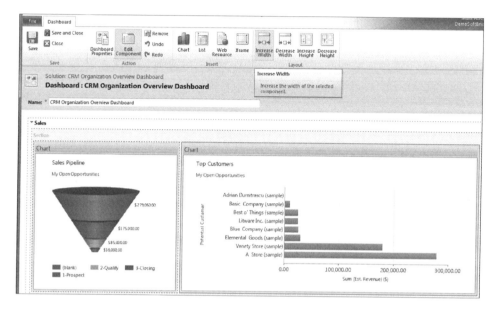

8. Scroll down if needed to select the second tab. Edit the tab component so that the label reads **Activities**.

9. Select the single component placeholder and adjust it using the **Decrease Width** button so it is only one cell wide.

10. Working with the same placeholder, add a chart. Select the **Activities by Month Due** chart using the **My Activities** view for the **Activity** entity, as shown in the following screenshot:

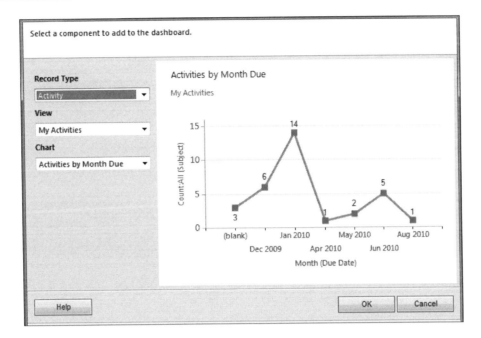

11. In the **Activities** tab, add a new list component. The list component should show the **My Activities** view for the **Activity** entity:

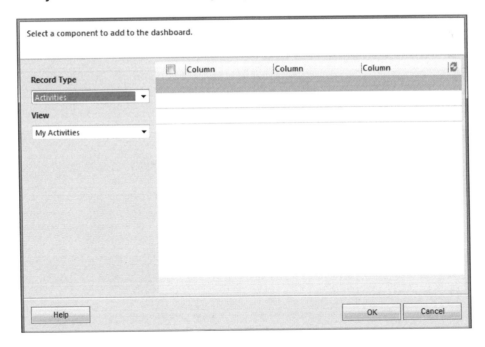

12. Move and adjust the width of the list component so that it fills the empty cells of the **Activities** tab:

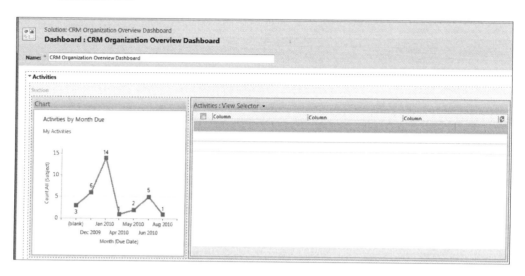

13. Scroll down and select the third tab. Edit the tab component and change the label to read **Service**. Select the first component placeholder and add a new chart. Select the **Case Mix (By Priority)** chart using the **My Active Cases** view for the **Case** entity, as shown in the following screenshot:

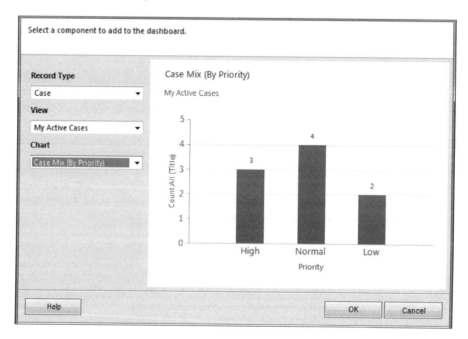

14. Adjust the new chart so that it only takes up one cell width.

15. Add a list component to the **Service** tab. The list component should show the **My Active Cases** view for the **Case** entity:

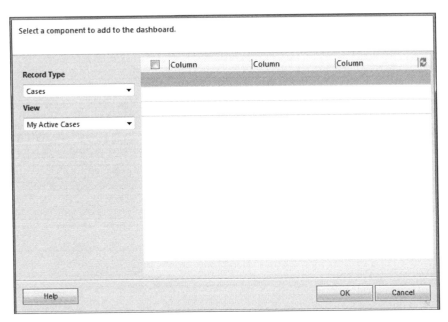

16. Move and adjust the list component so that it takes up two cell spaces in the tab:

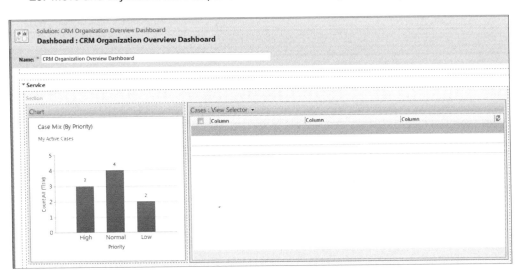

17. Once all of these changes have been made, click the **Save and Close** button in the dashboard editor toolbar area.

18. Locate the new dashboard in the solution package, select the record from the list and click the **Publish** button in the toolbar to make the changes available to the system users:

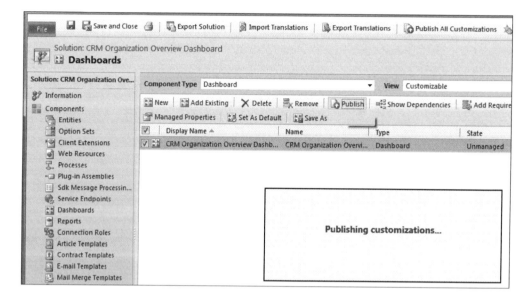

19. Once the publishing is complete, go to the main **Dashboards** area of the **Workplace** section in Dynamics CRM and select the new dashboard from the listing of system dashboards to view the results:

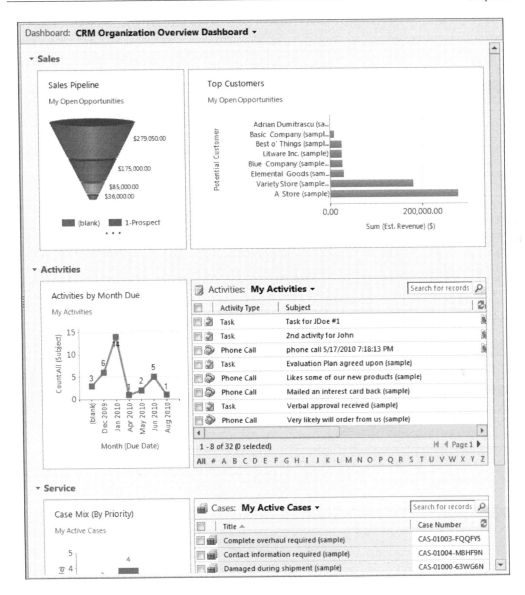

There's more...

Dynamics CRM has implemented certain limitations to how a dashboard layout can be modified. This section will identify a limitation, and ways to get around it.

Adding more than six components to a dashboard

The dashboards in Microsoft Dynamics CRM 2011 can only have a maximum of six dashboard components at a time. This is the total number of charts, lists, IFrames, and Web Resources combined.

If you are using Microsoft Dynamics CRM 2011 online, then you are stuck with this limitation. However, if you are using an on-premise version of Dynamics CRM 2011, your systems administrator can adjust the limit using a **Windows PowerShell** command. Please refer to the Microsoft Dynamics CRM SDK for the latest information about the syntax and steps involved in making this adjustment:

```
http://msdn.microsoft.com/en-us/library/gg334200.aspx
```

Performance Warning

Increasing the maximum number of dashboard components will affect both User and System dashboards. There is a performance trade-off where you may notice increased load on the system if you build dashboards with too many components that consume a high volume of data.

Installing the free Dashboard Reports control

Although it is possible to use an IFrame component on a Dynamics CRM dashboard to show an existing report, the team at Microsoft Dynamics Labs has released a free Dashboard Reports control for Microsoft Dynamics CRM 2011. Using this control instead of a standard IFrame creates a cleaner look to the final embedded report.

Getting ready

The **Dashboard Reporting Control** for Microsoft Dynamics CRM 2011 is freely available on the **Microsoft Dynamics Marketplace** website and works with both Dynamics CRM online and on-premise deployments. This recipe covers the steps to install and test the solution package.

How to do it...

Carry out the following steps in order to complete this recipe:

1. Navigate to the **Settings** area of Dynamics CRM 2011 Online. Go to the **Dynamics Marketplace** module located in the **Customizations** section. Once in the **Dynamics Marketplace** area, click on the **More Solutions** link, as shown in the following screenshot:

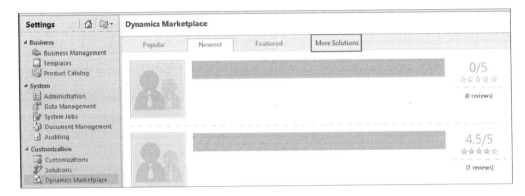

2. The **Microsoft Dynamics Marketplace** will open in a new browser window. Search for Dashboard Reporting Control. There should be one search result, as shown in the following screenshot:

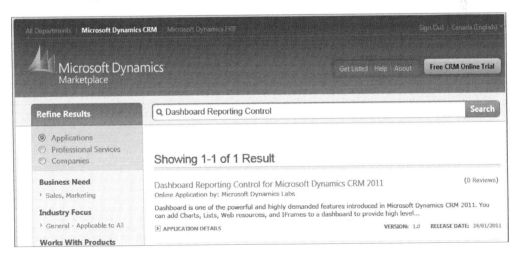

3. Clicking on the title of the solution will show the details screen. Click on the **Try It** button located in the upper-left corner to download the solution:

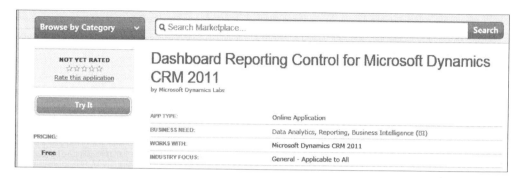

4. Once the solution file has been downloaded, navigate to the **Solutions** module in the **Settings** area and click on the **Import** button in the **Solutions** toolbar:

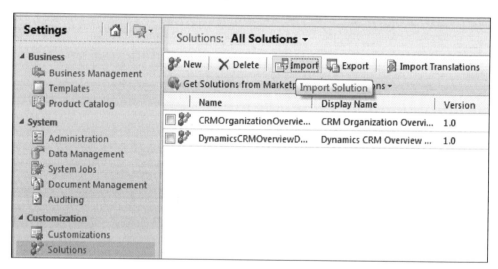

5. Click on the **Browse...** button and select the solution package `zip/` `cab` file that you downloaded earlier. The file will most likely be named `ReportcontrolforDashboard10man.zip.cab`, as shown in the following screenshot:

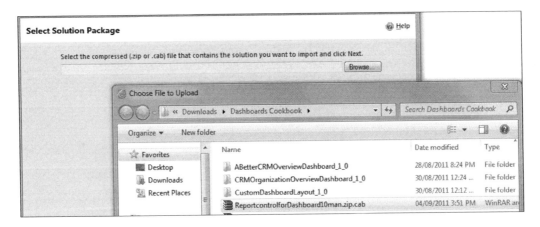

6. Once you have selected the solution package file, click on the **Next** button. Dynamics CRM will now validate the package contents. The **Solution Information** screen will appear; click on the **Next** button to continue. The import process will begin:

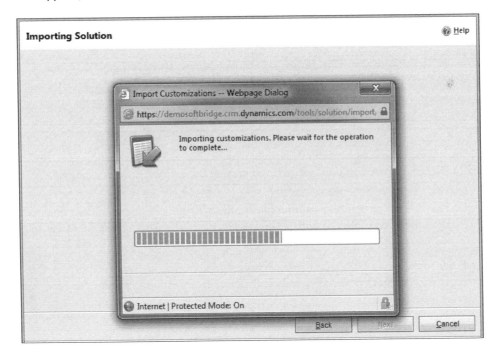

7. After the import has completed successfully, the **Importing Solution** screen will list all of the components included in the solution. Click the **Close** button to continue. Make sure to publish all customizations from the **Solution Explorer** dialog to ensure that your dashboard and the related components can be viewed later:

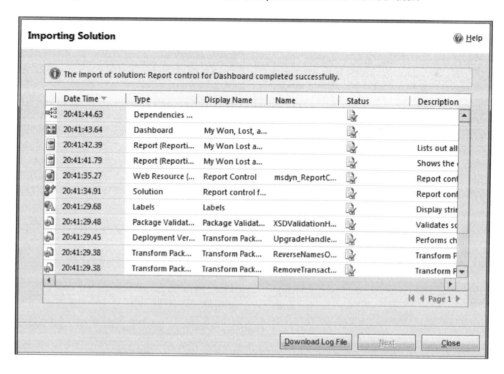

8. In order to make sure that the Report Control has been installed properly, go to the main **Dashboards** section of Dynamics CRM in the **Workplace** area.

9. View the list of available **Dashboards**, find and select the new dashboard named **My Won, Lost, and Open Opportunities**, as shown in the following screenshot. It should include a CRM report along with a list component showing Opportunity data:

How it works...

The free Dynamics CRM Dashboard Reporting control is part of a managed solution package. This solution will work for both Dynamics CRM online and on-premise deployments. The reporting control works with both User and System dashboards. The components included in the solution include the following:

Component Name	Type	Description
msdyn_ReportControl	Web Resource	This is an HTML web resource that uses some embedded JavaScript to read the `reportId` parameter, clean up the user interface, and present the rendered report in an IFrame.
My Won, Lost, and Open Opportunities	Report	The main report that takes the current UserId value as a parameter.

Component Name	Type	Description
My Won, Lost, and Open Opportunities for CustomerID	Report	Similar report, but targeted towards showing Opportunities base on the supplied CustomerID parameter. This would be good for form-level reporting.
My Won, Lost, and Open Opportunities	Dashboard	A dashboard that contains one `msdyn_ReportControl` and a list component.

There's more...

It is important to note that the Dynamics CRM Dashboard Reporting control has been designed to show reports that are currently hosted from Dynamics CRM. This means that only reports available in the Dynamics CRM reports listing can be shown using this control. The JavaScript functions that make up the `msdyn_ReportControl` are developed to show reports using the server URL and the `/crmreports/viewer/viewer.aspx` file that is part of the Dynamics CRM application.

In order to show non-CRM reports on the dashboard, the developer could simply use a standard IFrame dashboard component, or recreate the `msdyn_ReportControl` to handle outside reports if needed.

Showing reports on a Dynamics CRM dashboard

The previous recipe, *Installing the free Dashboard Reports control*, showed the reader how to install and test the CRM Dashboard Reporting control. This recipe will create a new User dashboard and add the reporting control while learning about the various features.

Getting ready

In order to complete this recipe, the user must have installed the Dashboard Reporting Control for Microsoft Dynamics CRM 2011 solution package as outlined in the previous recipe.

How to do it...

Carry out the following steps in order to complete this recipe:

1. Select the **Dashboards** link from the **Workplace** area and click on the **New** button to create a new User dashboard:

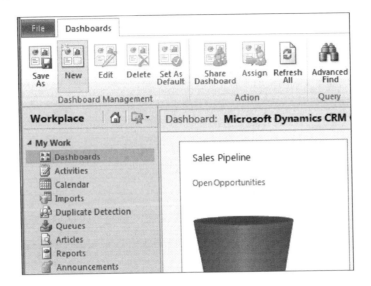

2. The **Select Dashboard Layout** dialog will appear; select the **3-Column Overview Dashboard** layout and click on the **Create** button, as shown in the following screenshot:

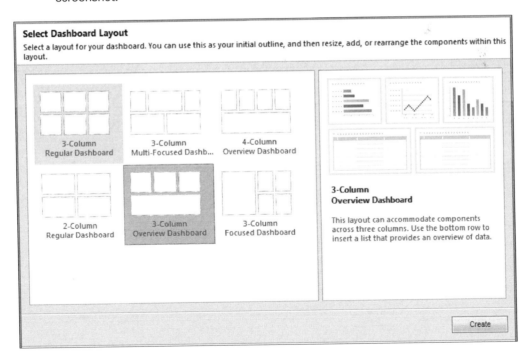

3. For the **Name** of the new dashboard, enter **Sales Pipeline Dashboard** and then click on the **Save** button:

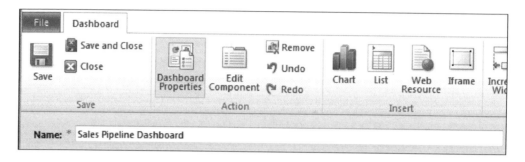

4. Customize the first tab of the dashboard by changing the label from **Tab** to **Charts**. Then, add three charts that show data related to the Sales module. Add the following charts for the Opportunity entity and base them on the **My Open Opportunities** view. The charts are: **Top Customers**, **Sales Pipeline**, and **Top Opportunities**. The dashboard should look like the following screenshot:

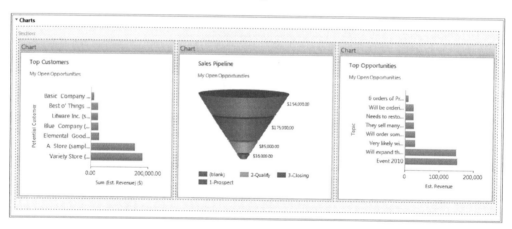

5. Move onto the second tab and change the label from **Tab** to **Report**. Add a web resource by clicking on the icon with the tool tip **Insert Web Resource** located in the component placeholder, as shown in the following screenshot:

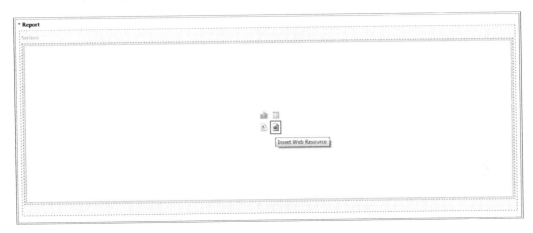

6. The **Add Web Resource** dialog will appear; click on the lookup button to search for available web resource components:

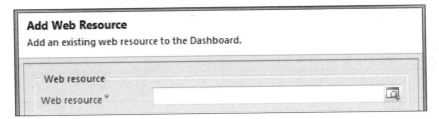

7. Locate the web resource named **msdyn_ReportControl**, select it, and click on the **OK** button to continue:

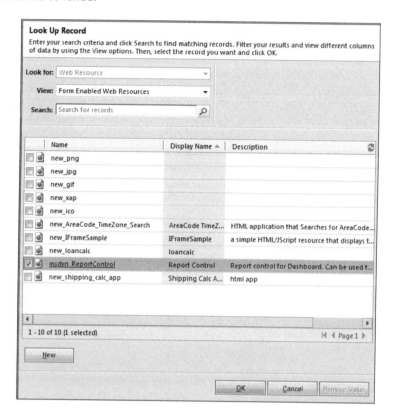

8. Back on the **Add Web Resource** dialog, make sure that the **Restrict cross-frame scripting** and **Pass record object-type code and unique identifier as parameters** options are not checked. Leave the **Custom Parameter(data)** textbox empty for now and click on the **OK** button. On the main **Dashboard Editor** screen, click on the **Save** button to commit all recent changes:

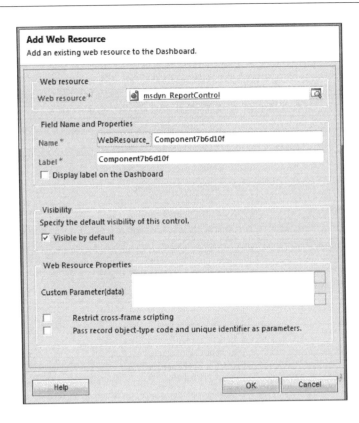

9. Now, we need to gather information about the report to display in the dashboard. Navigate to the **Reports** module in the **Workplace** area; locate and select the report named **Sales Pipeline** in the **Available Reports** view. Right-click on the record to show the **Options** menu, and click the **Copy a Link** menu item:

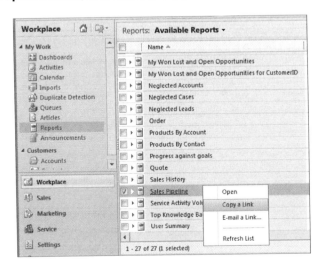

10. This next step will parse the copied link to get the unique report `id` needed for the dashboard component. Open up a simple text editor such as notepad and paste the string value that was copied from Dynamics CRM. The link should look something like the following (the `id` value will probably be different):

```
https://demosoftbridge.crm.dynamics.com/crmreports/viewer/
viewer.aspx?id=%7b51B73213-68F5-DE11-AB95-02BF0A0679D8%7d
```

11. From this long string value, copy the `id` value to your clipboard. The `id` value is located between the `%7b` and `%7d` character patterns. Based on the link in our example, we would only copy the following value to our clipboard:

```
51B73213-68F5-DE11-AB95-02BF0A0679D8
```

12. Navigate back to the new dashboard and edit the Report Control component. Paste the report `id` value into the **Custom Parameter(data)** field and click on the **OK** button, shown in the following screenshot:

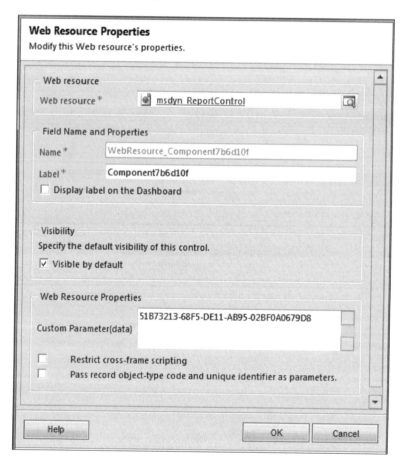

13. On the **Dashboard Editor** screen, click on the **Save and Close** button. Navigate to the **Dashboards** area in Dynamics CRM, locate the new **Sales Pipeline** dashboard and select it so that the results are displayed on the screen.

14. The report being displayed is fully interactive; you can adjust the report's filter settings and drill down into the charts, as shown in the following screenshot:

 Similar to using a standard IFrame, depending on the size of the report being shown, horizontal and vertical scroll bars will appear to help you navigate and view the report contents.

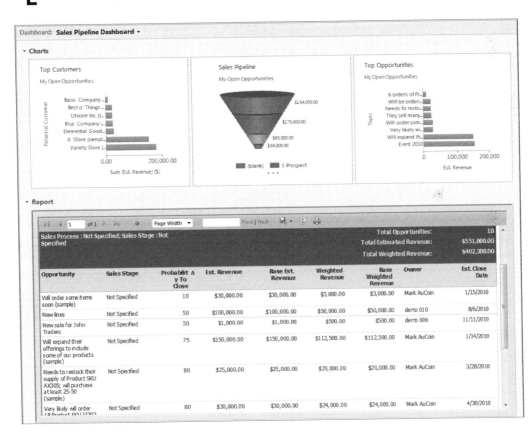

How it works...

The Reporting Control uses the report `id` value to determine which report to show on the dashboard. Once provided, it calls the standard `viewer.aspx` and shows it in an IFrame that has been tailored for viewing on a dashboard.

There's more....

There is no hard rule for placing a report on a dashboard. The user can have it stretched horizontal or vertical depending on their preference and the content of the report.

8
Creating a Chart

In this chapter, we will cover:

- ▶ Creating a system chart
- ▶ Creating a user chart
- ▶ Creating a stacked comparison chart
- ▶ Creating a multi-series chart

Introduction

Charts are referred to as **visualizations** in the Microsoft CRM SDK documentation. They provide the ability to graphically represent data being stored in Dynamics CRM. A CRM **entity** can have many different charts created for it. A chart can appear on a dashboard, as part of a list component, or even as a standalone control on a form.

This chapter is using the latest version of Dynamics CRM 2011, which includes the November 2011 update that has new charting features. For users of Dynamics CRM 2011 Online, the update is referred to as the R7 Update. For users of Dynamics CRM 2011 on-premises, the update is referred to as rollup #5. The items and steps outlined in this chapter require you to have the latest version of Dynamics CRM 2011 installed, either online or on-premises.

Creating a system chart

Many of the entities in Dynamics CRM come with predefined System charts. This recipe will show the reader how to create a new System chart that can be used as a visualization in Dynamics CRM.

Getting ready

This recipe is for users with the Administrator and/or System Customizer security roles. You will need to have access to the **Settings** area of Dynamics CRM.

How to do it...

Carry out the following steps in order to complete this recipe:

1. Navigate to the **Customization** section in the **Settings** area of Dynamics CRM. Click on the **Customize the System** link to open the default solution, as shown in the following screenshot:

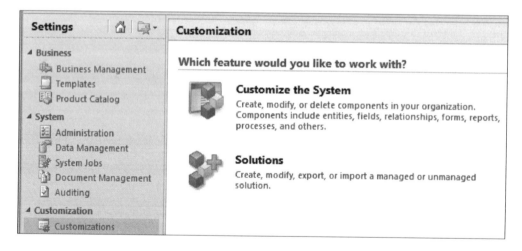

2. The **Solution Explorer** dialog showing the Default Solution for Dynamics CRM will open. Navigate through the **Entities** list and locate the **Case** entity. Within that entity, select the **Charts** link to see a listing of the available charts for the **Case** entity. Click on the **New** button in the toolbar to create a new chart:

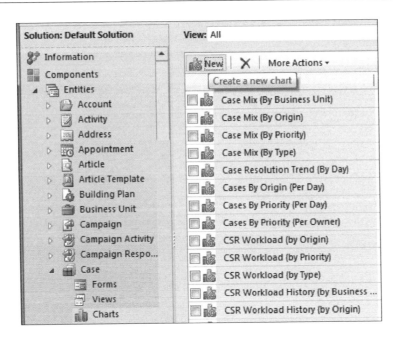

3. When the new chart dialog appears, specify the chart type by selecting the **Column** chart from the option set in the toolbar:

4. For the **View used for chart preview** field, select the **My Active Cases** view. The next field down is the chart name; type in **Cases by Priority**:

Working on solution: Default Solution
View used for chart preview
My Active Cases
Cases by Priority

5. The preview section of this dialog will be empty until the axis fields are set. In the **Legend Entries (Series)** list, select the **Priority** field. The aggregate setting should be set to **Count:All**. For the **Horizontal (Category) Axis Labels** field select the **Priority** field again, as shown in the following screenshot:

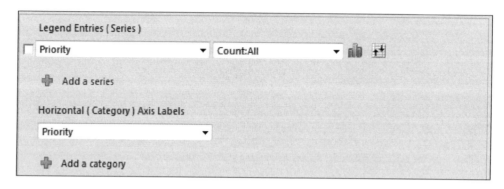

6. Once you are finished setting those parameters, the dialog will look similar to the following screenshot. You can provide a description if you want and then click on the **Save & Close** button to commit the changes:

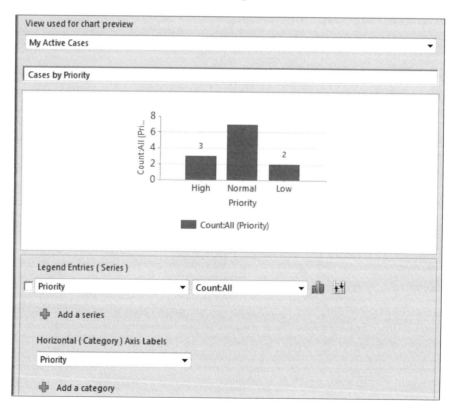

How it works...

The chart control being used in Microsoft Dynamics CRM is the same **Microsoft Chart Control** found in the Microsoft **.NET 3.5 Framework**. Charts are related to a Dynamics CRM entity and display data based on views related to the same entity. Charts can display data from both system views and user views. However, System charts cannot be rendered with a user view. The view being used for designing the chart can still be changed to another view when the chart is finally displayed on a dashboard or form.

CRM system views can be created using FetchXML or the SDK Query API; however, only views created using FetchXML can be used to render a system chart. This does not apply to User views because they can only be built using FetchXML in the built-in editor.

There's more...

Creating a chart with Dynamics CRM 2011 allows you to report on data that is provided from a view. Further, there are still more options available in the **Chart Designer** to further refine the data being visualized.

Using the Top/Bottom Rule options

When charting larger amounts of data, or when trying to focus on top or bottom sections of the data, a filter can be applied to the view by using the **Top X Rule** or **Bottom X Rule** parameters. Clicking on either of these toolbar buttons will let the designer pick from default filters or set a custom value. In order to turn the filter options off, click on the **Clear Rules** toolbar button:

Entities that support visualizations

The Microsoft Dynamics CRM SDK specifies that all **Custom Entities** and the following **System Entities** all support chart visualizations:

Account	Activity Pointer	Appointment	Bulk Operation	Campaign	Campaign Activity	Campaign Response
Competitor	Connection	Contact	Contract	Email	Fax	Goal
Goal Rollup Query	Incident	Invoice	Invoice Detail	KbArticle	Lead	Letter
List	Metric	Opportunity	Opportunity Product	Phone Call	Price Level	Product
Queue Item	Quote	Quote Detail	Recurring Appointment Master	Report	Sales Literature	Sales Order
Sales Order Detail	Service	Service Appointment	System User	Task	Team	Territory
UoM Schedule						

Creating a user chart

Creating charts in Dynamics CRM is not limited to only the Administrator and System Customizer security roles. Standard users of Dynamics CRM can also create User charts that are managed and viewed by the individual user. This recipe shows how a standard user can create a User chart.

Getting ready

In order for a non-admin user to create a User chart, they will need to have the User chart security privilege as part of their assigned CRM Security Role. Refer to the *There's more...* section of this recipe for further details.

How to do it...

Carry out the following steps in order to complete this recipe:

1. Start by navigating to the **Cases** section in the **Service** area of Dynamics CRM. You will see case records in the **My Active Cases** view. Now, along the top ribbon toolbar, click on the **Charts** tab, as shown in the following screenshot:

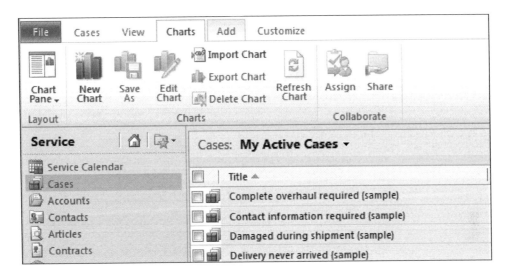

2. From the ribbon, click the **New Chart** button. A new tab will open on the ribbon, named **Chart Tools Design**. The **Chart Designer** will also appear on the right-hand side of the view pane:

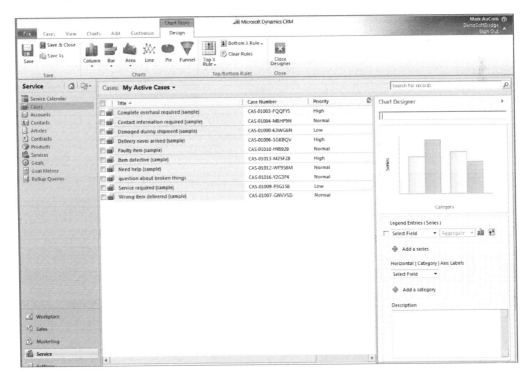

3. Provide a name for the chart; enter **My Cases by Priority Chart** into the first field of the **Chart Designer**.

4. In the **Legend Entries (Series)** section, select the **Priority** field and set the aggregate function to **Count:All**.

5. Next, select the chart type by clicking on the small chart icon sitting after the two fields you just completed. This will expand into a chart selection pop-up. Pick the standard **Column** chart option:

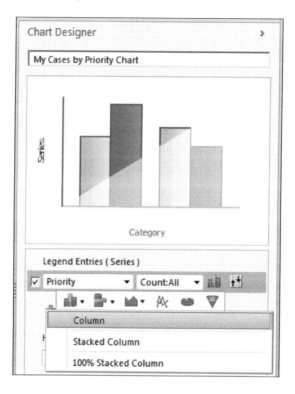

6. Moving onto the **Horizontal (Category) Axis Labels** field, select the **Priority** field from the list of options. The chart will now render in the preview window:

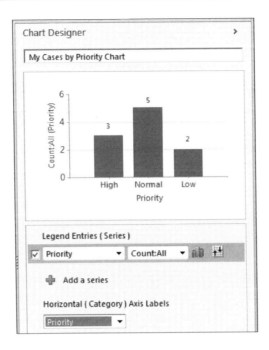

7. Now that the chart is finished, click the **Save & Close** button on the ribbon. This will close the **Chart Designer** and open the new User chart in the **Chart Pane** section of the list. You will also notice that many of the ribbon toolbar options are now enabled allowing you to manage the User chart:

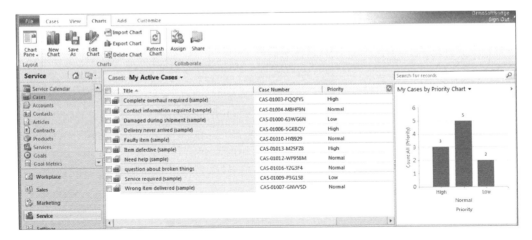

There's more...

Just like the differences between User dashboards and System dashboards, User charts have a few features unique to them that are not applicable to System charts.

Security Privileges needed to create user charts

In order for a user to create and manage a User chart, they will need to have a Dynamics CRM Security Role that at least has the **Create**, **Read**, and **Write** privileges for the **User Chart** entity. It is also worth noting that this entity only has two privilege settings of either **User** or **None Selected**:

Locating user charts

There is no central list of all the User charts that have been created by a user. In order to locate an existing User chart, you must first start with one of the views for the entity the chart was created for. When the Chart pane is showing, click on the list of available charts and scroll to the bottom of the list. The collection of User charts will be found there:

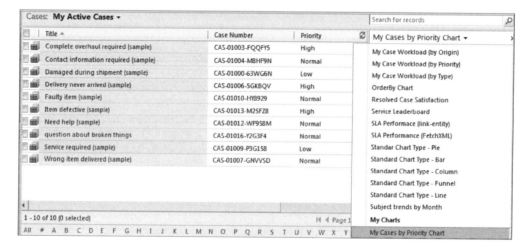

Editing a user chart

In order to edit an existing User chart, first locate the chart in the view (as mentioned in the previous section) and then switch to the **Charts** tab on the ribbon toolbar. If you have the proper security privileges, then you can click on the **Edit Chart** button to activate the **Chart Designer**, as shown in the following screenshot:

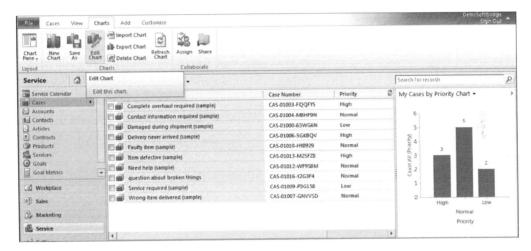

Assigning user charts

Unlike the CRM system charts, a User chart can be assigned to a different user. This will transfer the ownership of the Chart to a different CRM user. This is helpful when user charts are being constructed by the administration team, but need to be used by an individual who doesn't have the Create privilege (or doesn't want to build the chart).

When you have located the User chart and selected the **Charts** tab in the ribbon, as long as you have the Assign security privilege for User charts, then the **Assign** button will be available. Clicking on this button will launch the **Assign User Chart** dialog, which will allow you take control of the specific chart by selecting the **Assign to me** option.

Otherwise, you can pass the ownership of the chart to someone else (user or team) by selecting the **Assign to another user or team** option, and then filling in the value, as shown in the following screenshot:

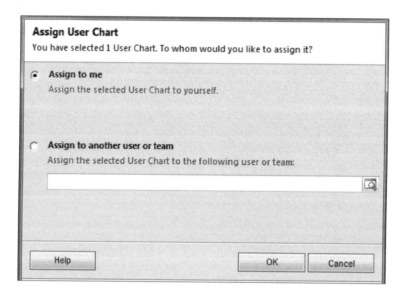

 When ownership is transferred from one user to another, the User chart is no longer available in the list of **My Charts** for the original user.

Sharing user charts

Similar to assigning charts to other users or teams, which transfers the ownership of the chart, there is also the option to share User charts in Dynamics CRM. Sharing a User chart literally allows you to share ownership with other users or entire teams in Dynamics CRM. The person sharing also gets the opportunity to specify how they would like to share the User chart and what privileges are being granted. This is often useful when a manager has created a chart that they want to share with their department (team) but not the entire company (all system users). The following shows the **Who would you like to share the selected user chart with?**, which allows you to share the selected chart with specific users with whom you want to share the chart:

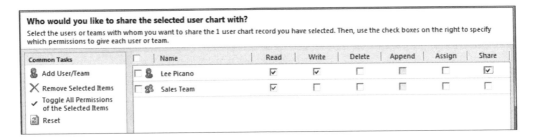

Creating a stacked comparison chart

Dynamics CRM 2011 offers flexible ways to visualize the CRM data using charts. One of the great charting features is the ability to easily create stacked comparison charts using the **Chart Designer** dialog.

Getting ready

This recipe assumes that the reader understands the basics of creating a chart. The techniques described here follow the creation of a System chart, but are the same when creating a User chart.

How to do it...

Carry out the following steps in order to complete this recipe:

1. Start by creating a new System chart based on the CRM Case entity. For information on how to create a chart you can refer to the *Creating a system chart* recipe or *Creating a user chart* recipe.

2. In the **Chart Designer** dialog, click on the **Column** icon in the **Charts** area of the toolbar and select **Stacked Column**, as shown in the following screenshot:

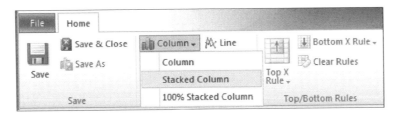

3. Select **My Active Cases** as the view used for chart preview. Provide a name for this new chart, such as **Cases Stacked by Priority and Type**.

4. In the **Legend Entries (Series)** section, select **Priority** as the series field, and **Count:All** as the aggregate function.

5. For the **Horizontal (Category) Axis Labels** section, select the **Priority** field again.

6. Next, click on the **Add a category** link. This will create the extra axis needed to complete the stacked comparison:

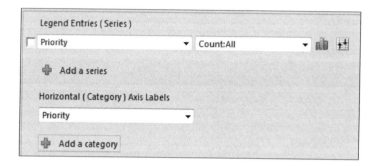

7. In the new category axis drop-down, select the **Case Type** field. The chart preview will now render and show you a stacked column chart:

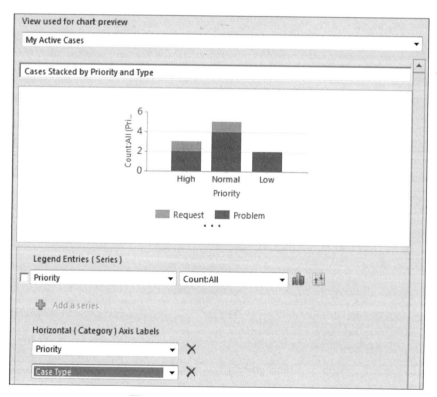

8. Click the **Save & Close** toolbar button to save the new chart.

There's more...

There are many different chart features available. The following section will provide more information about the stacked chart options.

Creating a 100% Stacked Column

In the previous recipe, we created a Stacked Column chart based on the Case entity. The Series axis was a counting of all the Cases by Priority, and they each had a different total count value. For some charting implementations, the individual count isn't the focus, but instead the stacking breakdown is more important. So, to show this type of chart, we would use the **100% Stacked Column** option. This will render a chart where the all the values of the series (Y axis) are scaled in percentages versus numeric counts:

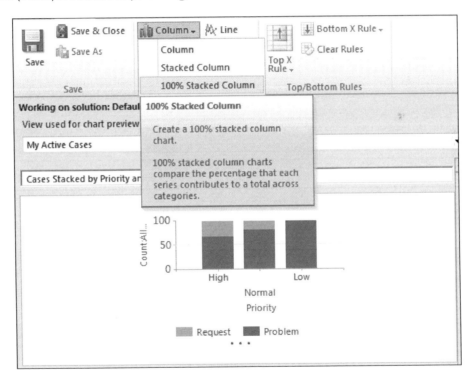

Chart types that support stacking

The Dynamics CRM **Chart Designer** dialog supports stacked and 100% stacked comparisons for the following chart types:

▸   Column type:

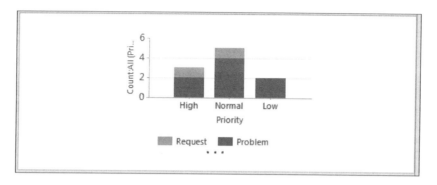

▸   Bar type:

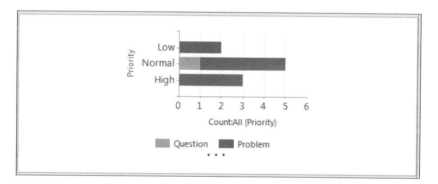

▸   Area type:

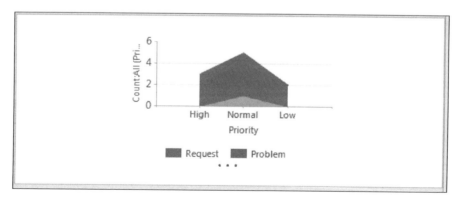

Creating a multi-series chart

When working with charts and reporting options, there is often a need to compare more than one series of data from the same record. A simple example of this is when comparing actual revenue versus estimated revenue for closed opportunities. In order to meet this need, Dynamics CRM supports using multiple series in charts.

Getting ready

This recipe assumes that the reader understands the basics of creating a chart. The techniques described here follow the creation of a System chart, but are the same when creating a user chart.

How to do it...

Carry out the following steps in order to complete this recipe:

1. Start by creating a new System chart based on the CRM Opportunity entity. For information on how to create a chart, refer to the *Creating a system chart* recipe or *Creating a user chart* recipe.

2. In the **Chart Designer** dialog, click on the **Column** icon in the **Charts** area of the toolbar and select the standard **Column** type.

3. For the chart name, use **Actual Revenue vs. Estimate Revenue by Probability**.

4. In the **Legend Entries (Series)** section, select the **Actual Revenue** field. Change the aggregate method to **Sum**.

5. Click on the **Add a series** link to create a new **Legend Entries (Series)** entry, as shown in the following screenshot:

6. Select the **Est. Revenue** field for the new entry.

7. Next, select the **Probability** field for the **Horizontal (Category) Axis Labels** option. The chart will render in preview mode showing you what the finished product will look like:

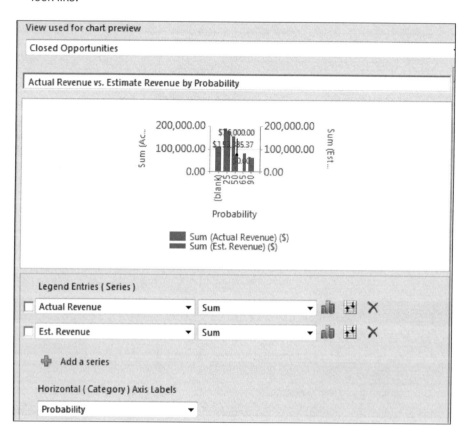

8. Click the **Save & Close** toolbar button to save the new multi-series chart.

There's more...

The chart prepared in this recipe used a two-series comparison. The following sections will describe some of the other options available for this type of chart.

Adding more series

The example in this recipe used a two-series comparison, but the **Chart Designer** can support up to five series. In order to add more series, simply click on the **Add a series** link again and then specify the field to chart on. In my example, I have a custom **Probability Adjusted Value** field that I used for the third series, as shown in the following screenshot:

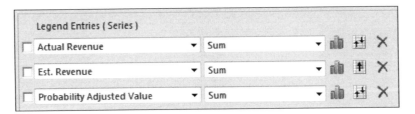

Set the Top/Bottom options for a series

Along with adding more series to the chart, you can also set the **Top/Bottom** option for each individual series. In order to set the **Top/Bottom** option for a series, click on the **Top/Bottom** icon located next to the series aggregate function. This will expand into the same menu options available from the main toolbar without having to first select the series using the selection checkbox:

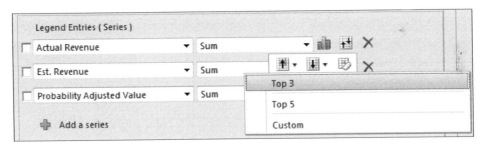

Changing the chart type for a series

Sometimes viewing the comparison data is easier when each series is represented in a different chart type. An example of this might be comparing actual revenue against estimated revenue by using a bar chart and line chart to see the differences. In order to change the chart type for a series, click on the chart icon located next to the aggregate drop-down. This will display a small menu that allows you to specify the display type to be used for each series in the chart, as shown in the following screenshot:

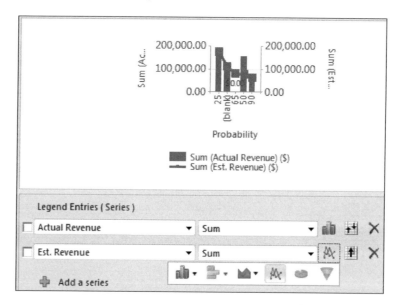

Removing a series

In order to remove a series from a multi-series or stacked comparison chart, simply click on the **X** icon located on the series line. This will remove the series and readjust the chart visualization:

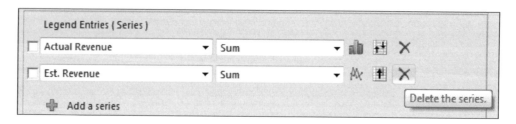

9

Advanced Chart XML

In this chapter, we will cover:

- ▶ Exporting a chart
- ▶ Importing a chart
- ▶ Changing Axis labels and Series label formats
- ▶ Controlling the chart colors and 3D appearance
- ▶ Using FetchXML to combine data in a chart

Introduction

Charts can be created using the Chart Designer tool in Dynamics CRM 2011. The chart tool has many great options and settings that can be applied; however, there are still limitations. This chapter will go into some of the advanced techniques used to modify and customize the charts used in Dynamics CRM 2011.

Exporting a chart

You do not need to create a new solution package to export a chart in Dynamics CRM 2011. However, following proper development standards means that you should have all custom charts included in a separate solution package once they have been customized. This recipe will use the **Export Chart** command to export charts from the CRM system to our local machine to make further customizations.

 The main part of this recipe shows how to export a System chart, and the *There's more...* section describes how to do the same for a user chart.

Getting ready

In order to export a System chart, you must be logged in as a System Administrator or have the Customizer Security Role.

How to do it...

Carry out the following steps in order to complete this recipe:

1. Navigate to the **Customization** section in the **Settings** area of Dynamics CRM. Click on the **Customize the System** link to open the default solution, as shown in the following screenshot:

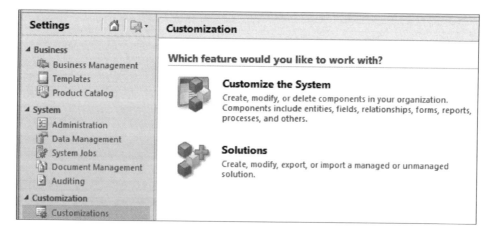

2. The **Solution Explorer** dialog showing the Default Solution for Dynamics CRM will open. Navigate through the **Entities** list and locate the **Case** entity. Within that entity, select the **Charts** link to see a listing of the available charts for the Case entity.

3. Create a new chart for the Case entity with the following parameters:

Property	Setting
View used for chart preview	My Active Cases
Name	Advanced Cases by Priority
Chart Type	Column
Series value	Case Number (Count:All)
Category value	Priority

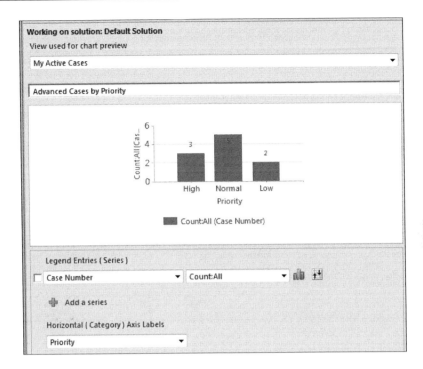

 Refer to *Chapter 8, Creating a Chart* if you are unsure about how to create a chart

4. Save and close the new chart to return to the listing of System Charts for the Case entity. Select your newly created chart from the list and click on the **Export Chart** option in the **More Actions** drop-down menu:

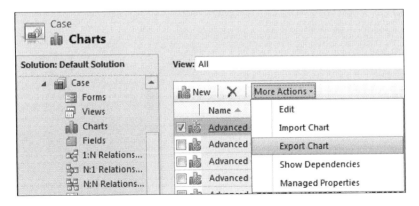

5. Dynamics CRM will download an XML file with the same name as your chart. Save the XML file to your local drive. This file will be used in the following recipes to extend the chart properties.

There's more...

Exporting a System chart requires that you have the proper system permissions such as Administrator or System Customizer Security Roles to get to the **Settings** area in the **Customization** section. After that you will need read and write privileges for the system chart entity. For user charts, if you have the read and write privileges for the User chart entity, then you will be able to export and import those charts as well.

Exporting a user chart

If you have created some user charts in the Dynamics CRM 2011 system, then you will also be able to export them and extend them. Start by creating a user chart for the Case entity (refer to *Chapter 8* for more details).

Locate your user chart and display it alongside a view in Dynamics CRM. The ribbon bar will enable the **Export Chart** button. Click on the **Export Chart** button and Dynamics CRM will prompt you to download an XML file. Save this XML file to your local drive. We will use this file in the following recipes to further extend the chart.

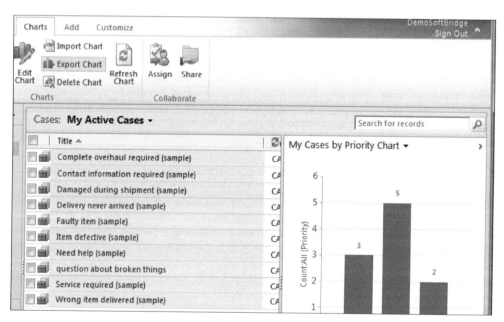

Importing a chart

If you have exported and edited a chart outside of Dynamics CRM, then you will need to import the chart back into Dynamics CRM before you can use it. This recipe includes the steps needed to import a chart back into Dynamics CRM.

 The main part of this recipe shows how to import a System chart, and the *There's more...* section describes how to do the same for a user chart.

Getting ready

In order to export a System chart, you must be logged in as a System Administrator or have the Customizer Security Role.

How to do it...

Carry out the following steps in order to complete this recipe:

1. Navigate to the **Customization** section in the **Settings** area of Dynamics CRM. Click on the **Customize the System** link to open the default solution.

2. Locate the **Case** entity in the left navigation of the **Solution Explorer** dialog. View the **Charts** listing for the entity and click on the **Import Chart** option in the **More Actions** menu, as shown in the following screenshot:

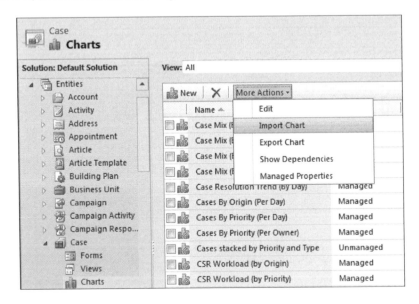

3. The **Import Chart** dialog will appear. Click on the **Browse** button to locate the XML file that was edited in the previous recipes. Once you have selected it, click the **OK** button to continue:

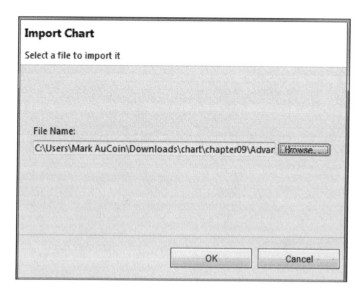

4. We are importing an existing chart (versus a brand-new one perhaps from another environment), and hence, Dynamics CRM will ask you how to handle the duplicate chart. Clicking on the **Replace** button will overwrite the original chart, while clicking on the **Keep Both** option will make a new chart with a unique name. For this recipe, click on the **Replace** button to continue:

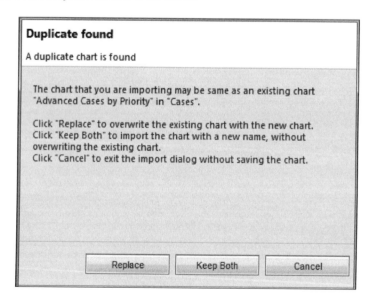

5. Assuming there are no errors with the chart that you are importing, the next screen will say that the chart was successfully imported. If there are errors with the XML, they will be noted on this screen. You can edit the Chart XML to fix the problems and try importing again. If there are no errors, then click on the **Close** button to continue:

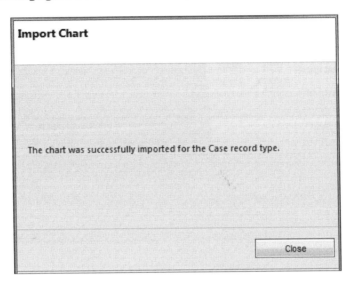

Import Chart

The chart was successfully imported for the Case record type.

Close

6. From the listing of charts shown in the **Solution Explorer**, locate the imported chart and double-click on **Open the Chart Designer** window. You will see a preview of what the modified chart will look like.

Remember to publish your customizations

In order to see the changes made by editing the Chart XML directly, make sure that you publish the owning entity after the chart is imported into the Dynamics CRM system.

There's more...

The following section covers the steps needed to import a user chart.

Importing a user chart

If you have created user charts in the Dynamics CRM 2011 system, and you have write permissions for the corresponding entity, then you will also be able to extend and re-import them. Assuming that you have already exported and extended a user chart for the Case entity (refer to *Chapter 8, Creating a Chart* for more details), then this section will show you how to import the modified chart back into Dynamics CRM.

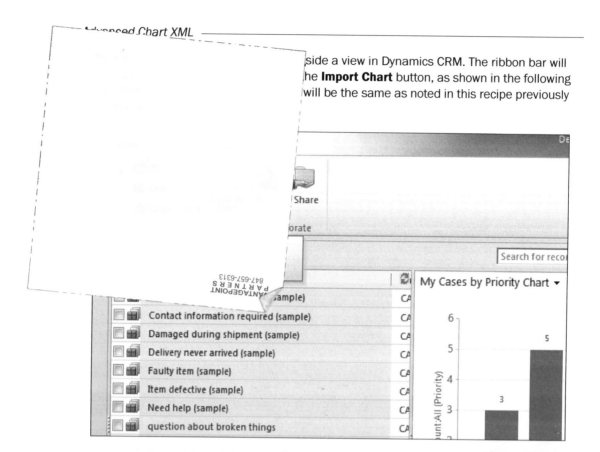

side a view in Dynamics CRM. The ribbon bar will
he **Import Chart** button, as shown in the following
will be the same as noted in this recipe previously

Changing Axis labels and Series label formats

This recipe will introduce you to some of the undocumented features available to the chart component in Dynamics CRM. When building a chart, Dynamics CRM will provide labels for the axis, but they are not the most user-friendly. This recipe will show you how to override those standard labels with something more meaningful along with setting formats for the Series data labels.

Getting ready

This recipe assumes that you are working with the chart created earlier in the *Exporting a chart* recipe. This chapter also assumes that the reader has access to an XML editor such as Microsoft Visual Studio.

How to do it...

Carry out the following steps in order to complete this recipe:

1. Locate the exported Chart XML file (either System chart or user chart) that was created in the earlier recipe. Open the XML file in the editor of your choice.

2. In order to change the axis labels, locate the `<AxisY>` element inside the `<ChartArea>` element. Add a new property to the element as follows:

Property	Value
Title	Total number of Cases

The following code demonstrates this:

```
<AxisY Title="Total number of Cases" LabelAutoFitMinFontSize="8"
TitleForeColor="59, 59, 59" TitleFont="{0}, 10.5px"
LineColor="165, 172, 181" IntervalAutoMode="VariableCount">
```

3. Locate the `<AxisX>` element as well, and add a new property to it as well.

Property	Value
Title	Grouped by Priority

The following code demonstrates this:

```
<AxisX Title="Grouped by Priority" LabelAutoFitMinFontSize="8"
TitleForeColor="59, 59, 59" TitleFont="{0}, 10.5px"
LineColor="165, 172, 181" IntervalAutoMode="VariableCount">
```

4. Locate the `<Series>` element and add a new property to set the format.

Property	Value
LabelFormat	F1

The following code demonstrates this:

```
<Series LabelFormat="F1" ChartType="Column"
IsValueShownAsLabel="True" Font="{0}, 9.5px"
LabelForeColor="59, 59, 59" CustomProperties="PointWidth=0.75,
MaxPixelPointWidth=40"></Series>
```

5. Save the changes made to the `.xml` file and import the chart back into Dynamics CRM (refer to the *Importing a chart* recipe for more details) to see the results. You will notice the Axis labels are different and the `LabelFormat` has changed from a single integer to a **Fixed-Point** format with one decimal place. This is shown in the following screenshot:

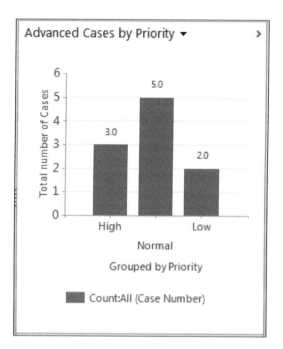

How it works...

The presentation description section of the Chart XML controls the appearance of the chart. There is no XML schema available to validate this section, but the Chart XML is a serialization of the Microsoft Chart Control from the Microsoft .NET 3.5 framework. Although not all of the properties are implemented, you can refer to the Microsoft Chart Control's `.chm` help file for more detailed information on the properties available. The following link will provide you with a download of the MS Chart control and the associated documentation:

`http://www.microsoft.com/download/en/details.aspx?id=11001`

There's more...

Understanding all of the different parameters and options available for extending charts in Dynamics CRM can take a long time. This section gives a quick overview of the **Chart XML Schema** along with some of the property settings for the data label formats.

Overview of the Chart XML Schema

The Chart XML shown in the `.xml` file exported from Dynamics CRM is editable, and can be modified to create results that cannot be modeled using the built-in chart designer in Dynamics CRM. The Chart XML Schema is made up of 2 main portions, each with its own important sub-sections. The other recipes in this chapter will each modify parts of the Chart XML to change the chart presentation. The Microsoft Dynamics CRM SDK provides detailed information around the Chart XML schema and all of the elements and attributes. The following is an overview of Chart XML:

```
<visualization>
  <datadescription>
    {...fetch xml...}
    {...charting columns...}
  </datadescription>
  <presentationdescription>
    {...chart series...}
    {...chart areas...}
    {...titles legends...}
  </presentationdescription>
</visualization>
```

Series LabelFormat options

Neither the MS Chart Control nor the Dynamics CRM 2011 documentation covers all of the formatting options available for the `LabelFormat` property. However, the Microsoft MSDN documentation does have a section on the overall .NET Framework formatting strings, which can be applied to the Chart control in Dynamics CRM 2011.

The following are some samples of common format strings that will work with the
`LabelFormat` property for Dynamics CRM 2011 chart controls:

Format String	Name	Description	Example using "123.45"
C or c	Currency	A numeric value is converted to a string that represents a currency amount.	$123.45
D or d	Decimal	Works only with integer values.	123
F or f	Fixed-Point	Converts the number into decimal format. Adding a precision value to the format will specify the number of decimal places.	123.45 "F1" equals 123.6
P or p	Percent	The number is converted into a string that represents a percent value. The precision value indicates the number of decimal places.	12,345 %

Format String	Name	Description	Example using "11/18/2011 2:30:44 PM"
d	Short Date	Shows a Short Date pattern that follows "MM/dd/yyyy".	11/18/2011
D	Long Date	Shows a Long Date pattern that follows "dddd, MMMM dd yyyy".	Friday, November 18, 2011
t	Short Time	Shows a Short Time pattern that follows "HH:mm".	2:30 PM
T	Long Time	Shows a Long Time pattern that follows "HH:mm:ss".	2:30:44 PM
M	Month	Shows a Month Day pattern that follows "MMMM dd".	November 18
Y	Year	Shows a Year pattern that follows "yyyy".	2011

These are some links to the online MSDN documentation that explain the following available
formats in more detail:

► Standard Numeric Format Strings:

    http://msdn.microsoft.com/en-us/library/dwhawy9k(v=VS.85).aspx

LabelFormat = "#0,#%" Label = "#PERCENT"

▶ Custom Numeric Format Strings:

`http://msdn.microsoft.com/en-us/library/0c899ak8(v=VS.85).aspx`

▶ Standard DateTime Format Strings:

`http://msdn.microsoft.com/en-us/library/az4se3k1(v=VS.85).aspx`

Controlling chart colors and 3D appearance

Building on the lessons learned earlier in the chapter, this recipe will show the reader how to change the colors used in the chart, along with setting up a 3D appearance. By default, Dynamics CRM automatically decides which colors to use for the chart; however, certain colors can mean different things depending on the audience. You may even wish to use a corporate color palette so that all charts look similar. By setting custom palettes and colors the developer has control over this option.

Getting ready

This recipe assumes that you are working with the chart created earlier in the *Exporting a chart* recipe. This chapter also assumes that the reader has access to an XML editor such as Microsoft Visual Studio.

How to do it...

Carry out the following steps in order to complete this recipe:

1. Locate the exported Chart XML file (either System chart or user chart) that was created in the earlier recipe. Open the XML file in the editor of your choice.

2. In the Chart XML, locate the `<Chart>` element located under the `<presentationdescription>` element.

3. Add the following two properties to the Chart element. This will override the default colors using a different shades of blue for the series.

Property	Value
Palette	None
PaletteCustomColors	55,118,193

The following code demonstrates this:

```
<Chart Palette="None" PaletteCustomColors="55,118,193">
```

4. If you want to, you can also turn off the **gradient color** feature, which is usually turned on by default. In order to turn it off, locate the `<Series>` element inside the `<Chart>` element and adjust the following property value:

Property	Value
`BackGradientStyle`	`None`

The following code demonstrates this:

```
<Series BackGradientStyle="None"
```

5. In order to be sure that the `Pallet` settings aren't overridden, you should also remove the `<Series>` element's `Color` and `BackSecondaryColor` properties if they are present.

6. In order to add the 3D affect to the chart, you need to add the `<Area3DStyle>` element before the `</ChartArea>` element's closing tag, shown as follows:

```
<Area3DStyle Enable3D="True" LightStyle="Simplistic" />
```

7. Save the changes and import the chart back into Dynamics CRM. The final chart should look similar to the following screenshot:

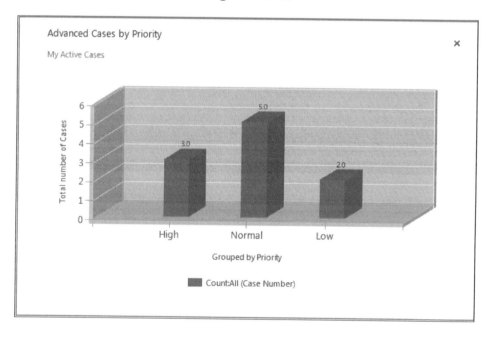

Controlling the color when dealing with multiple series

The example for controlling the color in this recipe showed how to set the base color when dealing with one data series only. If you have a chart that uses multiple data series then you can specify more than one color to use. There is also the option of using a predefined pallet as a property setting.

In order to specify more than one color using the `PalletCustomColors` property, simply list the different color options separated by a semicolon character. This code snippet specifies three different color options. The color options and the series work in parallel, meaning that the first series in the chart will get the first color listed, and so on:

```
PaletteCustomColors="55,118,193; 197,56,52; 149,189,66"
```

The MSDN documentation also specifies a set of predefined color pallets under the `CharColorPalette` Enumeration. These are noted in the following URL:

```
http://msdn.microsoft.com/en-us/library/system.web.
ui.datavisualization.charting.chartcolorpalette.aspx
```

Pallet Name	Description
Bright	Bright colors
Grayscale	Shades of black and white
Excel	Uses MS Excel-style colors
Pastel	Pastel colors
Berry	Blues and purples
Fire	Red, orange, and yellow colors

Options when using 3D styles

The MS Chart .NET 3.5 help file lists some of the properties available for customizing the 3D display settings of a chart. The following are some examples:

Property	Description	Options
LightStyle	Controls the lighting type	None, Realistic, Simplistic
Perspective	Integer value that represents the percent of perspective	Range between 0-100. Default is 0.
PointDepth	Integer value that controls the depth of data points	Range between 0-1000 percent. Default is 100.

Using FetchXML to combine data in a chart

The charts created and displayed in Dynamics CRM use the **FetchXML** syntax to query the underlying Dynamics CRM data source. Users can create comparison charts using the designer, but the comparisons are only based on one entity type. This recipe will create an **Account SLA** chart that shows how to manipulate the FetchXML query to pull and compare data from two different entities (Account and Case entities).

Getting ready

This recipe assumes that the reader has reviewed the earlier recipes and is familiar with how to export and import a chart from Dynamics CRM. This recipe will require you to add custom fields to the Account entity and make sure there are some active Case records related to active Accounts.

How to do it...

Carry out the following steps in order to complete this recipe:

1. Navigate to the **Customization** section in the **Settings** area of Dynamics CRM. Click on the **Customize the System** link to open the default solution, as shown in the following screenshot:

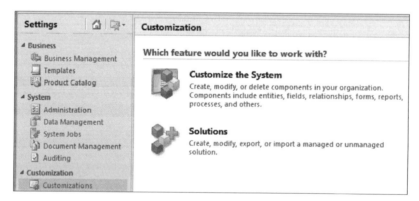

2. In the **Solution Explorer** dialog, navigate to the **Account** entity and create a custom **Service Units SLA** field with the following properties:

Property	Value
Display Name	**Service Units SLA**
Name	new_serviceunitssla
Requirement Level	No Constraints
Type	Whole Number

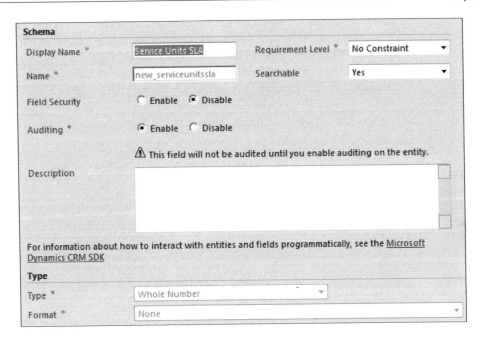

3. Save this new field and add it to the **Account** form. Now, publish the changes:

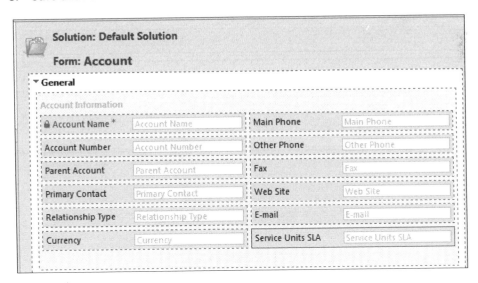

4. In the **Solution Explorer**, navigate to the **Case** entity, edit the form, and make sure that the **Billed Service Units** field is being displayed. Note that the Billed Service Units field is a standard field included with Dynamics CRM, simply not shown on the **Case** form as part of the default deployment:

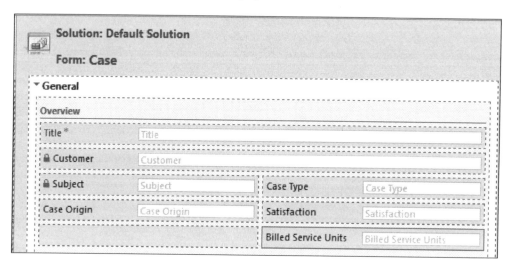

5. Save the changes and publish the customizations.

6. Now that the fields are ready and being displayed, you will need to edit the active Account records and provide values for the new **Service Units SLA** field. For this example, use values in the range of **7** to **10**.

7. After updating the Account records, open the active Case records and provide values for the **Billed Service Units** field. For this example, provide a range of numbers between **2** and **12**. This will result in some Cases being below the SLA level and some being above the SLA level.

8. We are ready to make the basic chart now. In the **Solution Explorer** dialog, navigate to the **Case** entity and create a new System chart using the following parameters:

Property	Value
View used for chart preview	My Active Cases
Name	Account SLA Performance
Chart Type	Column
Legend Entries (Series)	Billed Service Units (Sum)
Horizontal (Category) Axis Labels	Customer

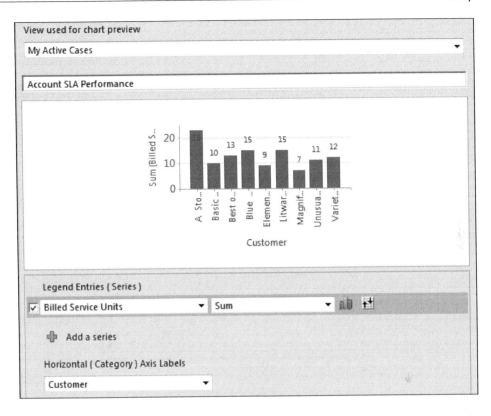

9. Save the chart and export it to your local drive. We will modify it further in the next few steps.

10. Once the chart is exported, open the Chart XML file in an XML editor such as Microsoft Visual Studio and locate the `<fetch>` segment near the top of the file:

```
<fetch mapping="logical" aggregate="true">
  <entity name="incident">
    <attribute groupby="true" alias="_CRMAutoGen_groupby_column_
Num_0" name="customerid" />
    <attribute alias="_CRMAutoGen_aggregate_column_Num_0"
name="billedserviceunits" aggregate="sum" />
  </entity>
</fetch>
```

11. Adjust the `<fetch>` segment by adding a `<link-entity>` condition that pulls in data from the Account entity's **Service Unit SLA** field, shown as follows:

```
<fetch mapping="logical" aggregate="true">
  <entity name="incident">
     <attribute groupby="true" alias="_CRMAutoGen_groupby_column_
Num_0" name="customerid" />
     <attribute alias="_CRMAutoGen_aggregate_column_Num_0"
name="billedserviceunits" aggregate="sum" />
     <link-entity name="account" from="accountid" to="customerid"
alias="ab">
        <attribute name="new_serviceunitssla" alias="aggregate_
column2" aggregate="max" />
     </link-entity>
  </entity>
</fetch>
```

12. Now that a new field has been included in the `FetchXML`, we can add it to the `<measurecollection>`, so that it is included in the calculations:

```
<category alias="_CRMAutoGen_groupby_column_Num_0">
  <measurecollection>
     <measure alias="_CRMAutoGen_aggregate_column_Num_0" />
  </measurecollection>
  <measurecollection>
     <measure alias="aggregate_column2" />
  </measurecollection>
</category>
```

13. Next, we set up a new **Line** chart in red to display the Account's Service Unit Agreement value against the Case's Billed Service Units results shown in the existing column chart:

```
<Series>
   <Series ChartType="Column" IsValueShownAsLabel="True" Font="{0},
9.5px" LabelForeColor="59, 59, 59" CustomProperties="PointWid
th=0.75, MaxPixelPointWidth=40" />
   <Series ChartType="Line" CustomProperties="PointWid
th=0.75, MaxPixelPointWidth=40" LabelForeColor="59, 59, 59"
Font="{0}, 9.5px" BackGradientStyle="None" Color="255,0,0"
IsValueShownAsLabel="False"/>
</Series>
```

14. Now that all of those changes have been made to the Chart XML, import the chart and you will see the final results, as shown in the following screenshot. Note that the results may vary depending on the amount of data you have in your system:

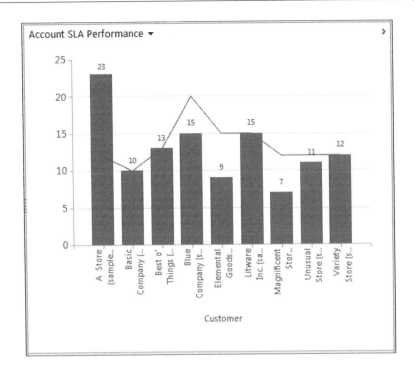

There's more...

This recipe covered some of the basics around using FetchXML to specify what data is being combined in a chart. The following URL to the Microsoft MSDN library provides more detailed information along with examples on how to use FetchXML:

http://msdn.microsoft.com/en-us/library/gg328332.aspx

Using Advanced Find to generate FetchXML

Learning all the syntax conditions around FetchXML can be fun for some people. There is a much easier way to build FetchXML queries in Dynamics CRM 2011 using the **Advance Find** query tool.

Launch the **Advanced Find** dialog in Dynamics CRM and build a query that pulls the data that you wish to see in your chart. This can also include data from multiple entities, similar to what we did earlier in this recipe. Once you have tested the query and found the results that you are looking for and edit the column layout to include the fields you need, click on the **Download Fetch XML** button in the **Advanced Find** ribbon toolbar, as shown in the following screenshot:

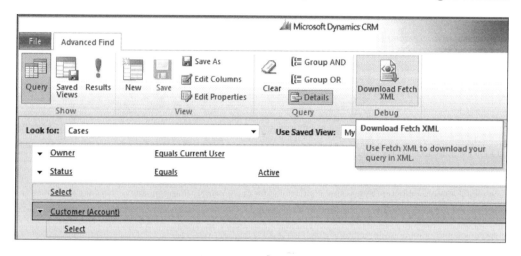

Clicking on that button will download a `FetchXML` file that you can then use to replace or augment the `FetchXML` query being used by your CRM chart:

```xml
<fetch version="1.0" output-format="xml-platform" mapping="logical"
distinct="false">
  <entity name="incident">
    <attribute name="incidentid" />
    <attribute name="billedserviceunits" />
    <attribute name="customerid" />
    <order attribute="billedserviceunits" descending="false" />
    <filter type="and">
      <condition attribute="ownerid" operator="eq-userid" />
      <condition attribute="statecode" operator="eq" value="0" />
    </filter>
    <link-entity name="account" from="accountid" to="customerid"
alias="aa">
      <attribute name="new_serviceunitssla" />
    </link-entity>
  </entity>
</fetch>
```

Dashboard Examples

The appendix for this book includes two dashboards that use some advanced `ChartXML` and `FetchXML` to build charts that you don't find out-of-the-box with Dynamics CRM. Hopefully, they will be useful and provide you with ideas of your own to extend the charting and dashboard experience. The two dashboards that we will be looking at are:

- ▶ Sales Dashboard
- ▶ Service Dashboard

Sales Dashboard

Instead of showing the standard out-of-the-box charts on a sales dashboard, this chapter will show some new custom-built charts using the techniques mentioned in *Chapter 9, Advanced Chart XML*. The list control on the dashboard is just a simple view of the user's **Open Activities** records, as shown in the following screenshot:

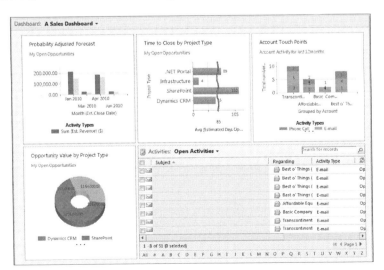

Probability Adjusted Forecast

The **Probability Adjusted Forecast** visualization uses a multi-series column chart to report on open **Opportunity** records. As shown in the following screenshot, the first series (in blue) is the **Estimated Revenue Value**. The second series (in yellow) is a custom field added to the Opportunity entity named **Probability Adjusted Value**. Since FetchXML is not able to generate calculated fields, (such as the Probability Adjusted Value), a workflow was built that is triggered when the Estimated Revenue Value or Probability fields change, and recalculates the Probability Adjusted Value. Some of the Opportunity charts that come standard with Dynamics CRM allow you to compare Estimated vs. Actual revenue values. However, this is an example of how a multi-series chart can compare other values as well, including custom fields:

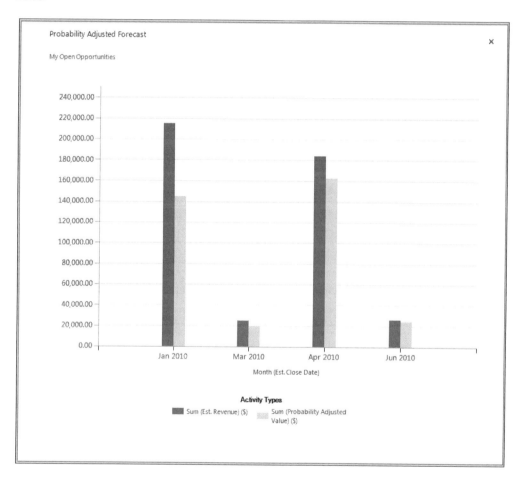

Time to Close by Project Type

The **Time to Close by Project Type** visualization is a bar chart that groups Opportunities by a custom **Project Type** option set and calculates the average **Estimated Days Open** field. The custom **Estimated Days Open** field is the difference between the Created Date and Estimated Close Date values. The idea was to show the average of how long each of these project types takes to close. The chart uses the optional `ScaleBreakStyle` element in the Chart XML to better present the data by avoiding large gaps when there are big differences in the data. This element goes into the `AxisY` element in the Chart XML:

```
<ScaleBreakStyle Enabled="True" BreakLineStyle="Wave" Spacing="2"
CollapsibleSpaceThreshold="50" />
```

There are some interesting parameters available to help customize this option. In this example a **Wave** style was used with a threshold of **50**, which means if there is a difference in bar values greater than 50%, show a scale break that looks like a wave. This is shown in the following screenshot:

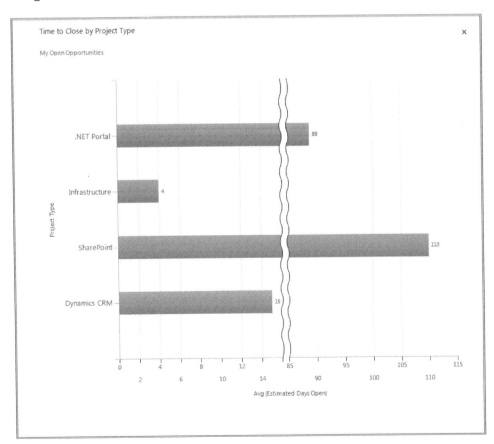

Account Touch Points

The **Account Touch Points** visualization uses a stacked bar chart, similar to the chart shown in *Chapter 8, Creating a Chart* to show how many Activities have been tracked against the salesperson's accounts over the last 12 months. The Y Axis counts the total number of Activities, where the X axis groups by account and then stacks by Activity type (filtered on phone calls, e-mails and appointments), as shown in the following screenshot:

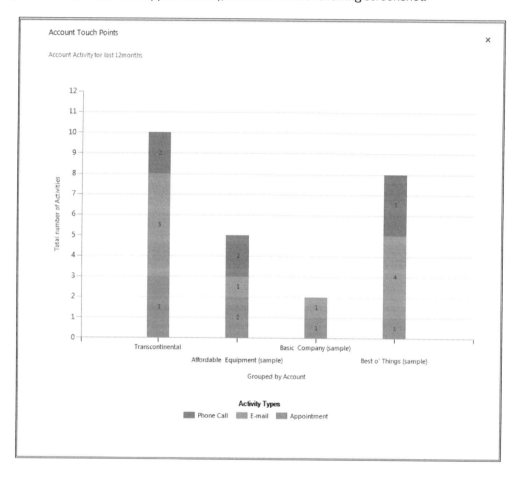

Opportunity Value by Project Type

The **Opportunity Value by Project Type** visualization is a 3D doughnut chart that groups open Opportunities by the custom **Project Type** option set field, as shown in the following screenshot:

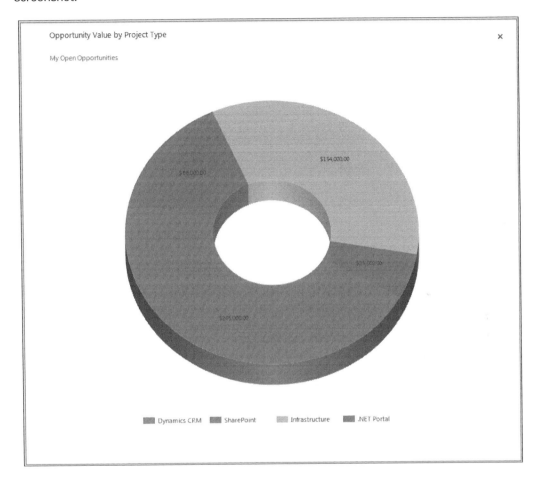

Service Dashboard

Microsoft Dynamics CRM comes standard with some excellent service-module dashboards and charts that let the user view data in many different ways. My take on the Service Dashboard is around trending and **Service Level Agreements** (**SLA**). There is a list included on the dashboard to let the service representative get access to open work items. The following screenshot shows a Service Dashboard:

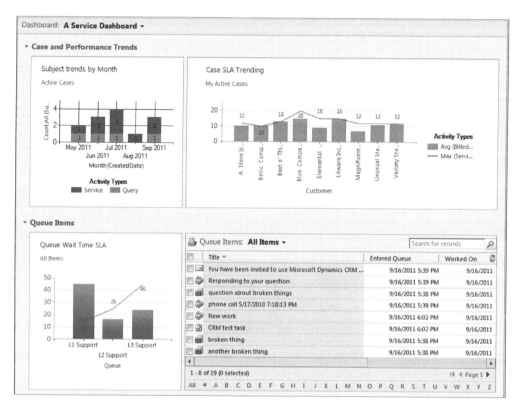

Subject trends by Month

The **Subject trends by Month** visualization uses a stacked column chart showing total case counts, grouped by month, and stacked by the **Subject** field, as shown in the following screenshot. This sample only has two different subjects, but if you were to use a more elaborate subject tree, perhaps something such as shipping, manufacturing, and billing, the results would allow you to see growing trends in different Case subjects:

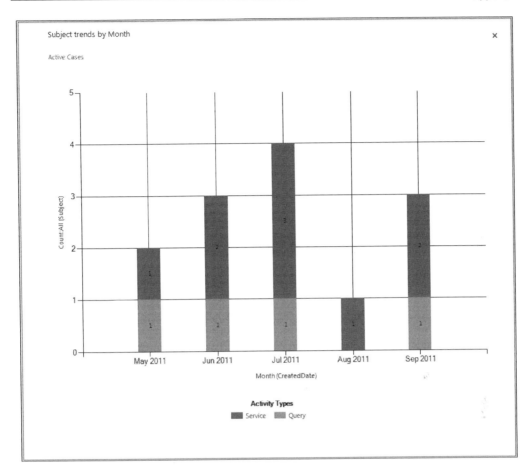

Case SLA Trending

The **Case SLA Trending** visualization is a multi-series chart that uses the bar graph to show the average number of **Billed Service Units** against an Account, while the line graph shows the **Service Units SLA** number for the Account. This chart lets an account manager or service manager get an idea of how they are doing compared to the SLA they have with each account. In order to implement this chart, a custom field named `serviceunitssla` is added to the `Account` entity, as shown in the following code snippet. The trick was to include this field by using a `<link-entity>` parameter in the chart's `FetchXML` statement to pull the SLA value from the Account record related to the main Case (incident) entity that the chart is based on. More information about `FetchXML` is available in *Chapter 9, Advanced Chart XML*:

```
<fetch mapping="logical" aggregate="true">
 <entity name="incident">
  <attribute alias="aggregate_column" name="billedserviceunits"
aggregate="avg" />
```

```
<link-entity name="account" from="accountid" to="customerid"
visible="false" link-type="outer" alias="a_4b5945b8a4a64613afc1ae1d5e
6828c7">
    <attribute alias="aggregate_column2" name="new_serviceunitssla"
aggregate="max" />
  </link-entity>
  <attribute groupby="true" alias="groupby_column" name="customerid"
/>
 </entity>
</fetch>
```

The following screenshot demonstrates the changes:

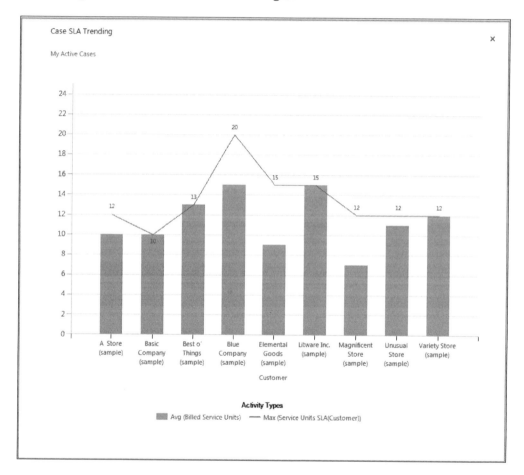

Queue Wait Time SLA

The **Queue Wait Time SLA** visualization is another multi-series chart that uses the bar graph to display the average wait time (in minutes) that an item sits in a **queue** before being assigned to someone directly. These **queue items** are grouped by queue, and the line graph shows the wait time SLA assigned to each queue. For example, the **L1 Support** queue has a **Queue Wait Time SLA** of **15** minutes, but the chart shows that they are averaging about **45** minutes (which is not good). In a similar approach to that mentioned for the chart earlier, this FetchXML uses a `<link-entity>` parameter to pull the SLA from a related entity:

```
<fetch mapping="logical" aggregate="true">
 <entity name="queueitem">
  <attribute alias="aggregate_column" name="new_waittime"
aggregate="avg" />
  <link-entity name="queue" from="queueid" to="queueid"
visible="false" link-type="outer" alias="a_4b5945b8a4a64613afc1ae1d5e
6828c7">
    <attribute alias="aggregate_column2" name="new_waittimesla"
aggregate="max" />
  </link-entity>
  <attribute groupby="true" alias="groupby_column" name="queueid" />
  </entity>
</fetch>
```

The following screenshot demonstrates the changes:

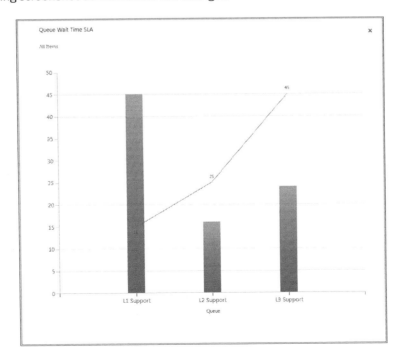

Index

Thank you for buying
Microsoft Dynamics CRM 2011: Dashboards Cookbook

About Packt Publishing

Packt, pronounced 'packed', published its first book "*Mastering phpMyAdmin for Effective MySQL Management*" in April 2004 and subsequently continued to specialize in publishing highly focused books on specific technologies and solutions.

Our books and publications share the experiences of your fellow IT professionals in adapting and customizing today's systems, applications, and frameworks. Our solution-based books give you the knowledge and power to customize the software and technologies you're using to get the job done. Packt books are more specific and less general than the IT books you have seen in the past. Our unique business model allows us to bring you more focused information, giving you more of what you need to know, and less of what you don't.

Packt is a modern, yet unique publishing company, which focuses on producing quality, cutting-edge books for communities of developers, administrators, and newbies alike. For more information, please visit our website: www.PacktPub.com.

About Packt Enterprise

In 2010, Packt launched two new brands, Packt Enterprise and Packt Open Source, in order to continue its focus on specialization. This book is part of the Packt Enterprise brand, home to books published on enterprise software – software created by major vendors, including (but not limited to) IBM, Microsoft and Oracle, often for use in other corporations. Its titles will offer information relevant to a range of users of this software, including administrators, developers, architects, and end users.

Writing for Packt

We welcome all inquiries from people who are interested in authoring. Book proposals should be sent to author@packtpub.com. If your book idea is still at an early stage and you would like to discuss it first before writing a formal book proposal, contact us; one of our commissioning editors will get in touch with you.

We're not just looking for published authors; if you have strong technical skills but no writing experience, our experienced editors can help you develop a writing career, or simply get some additional reward for your expertise.

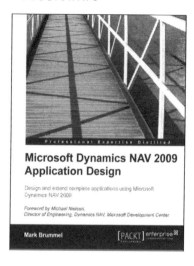

Microsoft Dynamics NAV 2009 Application Design

ISBN: 978-1-84968-096-7   Paperback: 496 pages

A focused book and ebook tutorial for Microsoft Dynamics NAV application development

1. Learn how Dynamics NAV ERP suite is set up and customized for various industries

2. Integrate numerous parts of a company's operations including financial reporting, sales, order management, inventory, and forecasting

3. Develop complete applications and not just skeleton systems

4. Covers the design and implementation of two new add-on services: The Squash application and the Storage & Logistics application

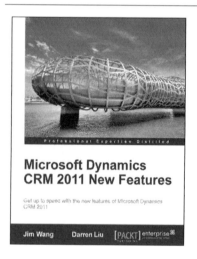

Microsoft Dynamics CRM 2011 New Features

ISBN: 978-1-84968-206-0   Paperback: 288 pages

Get up-to-speed with the new features of Microsoft Dynamics CRM 2011 with this Dynamics CRM

1. Master the new features of Microsoft Dynamics 2011

2. Use client-side programming to perform data validation, automation, and process enhancement

3. Learn powerful event driven server-side programming methods: Plug-Ins and Processes (Formerly Workflows)

4. Extend Microsoft Dynamics CRM 2011 in the Cloud

Please check **www.PacktPub.com** for information on our titles

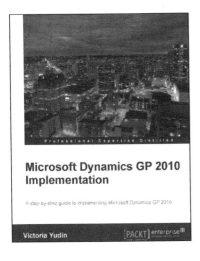

Microsoft Dynamics GP 2010
Implementation

A step-by-step guide to implementing Microsoft Dynamics GP 2010

Victoria Yudin   [PACKT] enterprise ⌗

Microsoft Dynamics GP 2010 Implementation

ISBN: 978-1-84968-032-5   Paperback: 376 pages

A step-by-step book and eBook guide to implementing Microsoft Dynamics GP 2010

1. Master how to implement Microsoft Dynamics GP 2010 with real world examples and guidance from a Microsoft Dynamics GP MVP

2. Understand how to install Microsoft Dynamics GP 2010 and related applications, following detailed, step-by-step instructions

3. Learn how to set-up the core Microsoft Dynamics GP modules effectively

4. Discover the additional tools available from Microsoft for Dynamics GP

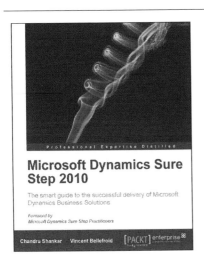

Microsoft Dynamics Sure
Step 2010

The smart guide to the successful delivery of Microsoft Dynamics Business Solutions

Foreword by
Microsoft Dynamics Sure Step Practitioners

Chandru Shankar   Vincent Bellefroid   [PACKT] enterprise ⌗

Microsoft Dynamics Sure Step 2010

ISBN: 978-1-84968-110-0   Paperback: 360 pages

The smart guide to the successful delivery of Microsoft Dynamics Business Solutions using Microsoft Dynamics Sure Step 2010

1. Learn how to effectively use Microsoft Dynamics Sure Step to implement the right Dynamics business solution with quality, on-time and on-budget results.

2. Leverage the Decision Accelerator offerings in Microsoft Dynamics Sure Step to create consistent selling motions while helping your customer ascertain the best solution to fit their requirements

Please check **www.PacktPub.com** for information on our titles